Thank you, Canada.

Life After America is dedicated to everyone who has ever imagined leaving their country and starting over someplace else, and to my love, Joanie Shirriff.

"I speak to you tonight in a spirit of hope. Eighteen years ago [1945] the advent of nuclear weapons changed the course of the world as well as the war. Since that time, all mankind has been struggling to escape from the darkening prospect of mass destruction on earth. In an age when both sides have come to possess enough nuclear power to destroy the human race several times over, the world of communism and the world of free choice have been caught up in a vicious circle of conflicting ideology and interest. Each increase of tension has produced an increase of arms; each increase of arms has produced an increase in tension."

—Excerpt from President John F. Kennedy's speech
to the world on July 26, 1963 announcing the Nuclear Test Ban Treaty,
the first serious mini-step to roll back the nuclear threat of Armageddon
for future generations, and four months before Kennedy was assassinated.

"We travel together, passengers on a little spaceship, dependent upon its vulnerable reserves of air and soil, all committed for our safety to its security and peace; preserved from annihilation only by the care, the work, and, I will say, the love we give our fragile craft. We cannot maintain it half fortunate, half miserable, half confident, half despairing, half slave to the ancient enemies of man, half free in a liberation of resources undreamed of until this day. No craft, no crew can travel safely with such vast contradictions. On their resolution depends the survival of us all."

—Excerpt from the speech of Adlai Stevenson II,
US Ambassador to the United Nations, on July 9, 1965
to the UN Economic and Social Council, Geneva, Switzerland,
five days before his death.

CHAPTER 1

November 10, 1967

CRAZY THOUGHTS FLASHED through my mind as my plane touched down at Dorval Airport on the outskirts of Montreal. I felt incapable of separating paranoia from reality.

Does the FBI know what I'm doing? Have they already picked up my trail? Am I on some government list?

What the hell am I doing running away? Shouldn't I stay and face the consequences?

Three weeks before my escape, I was living a carefree life in one of the canyons in the Hollywood Hills, trying to get closer to a kind, beautiful, intelligent woman named Jennifer, and thinking about ways to fix my first novel.

Three weeks later, I was a fugitive committing a felony.

I helped the smartly dressed, older woman beside me retrieve her bag from the overhead compartment.

It was the least I could do after making a point of not wanting to talk during the flight.

I am a writer, I reminded myself as I followed the other passengers through the airport toward customs and immigration. My only job is to survive and record. Like Henry David Thoreau. Like John Steinbeck, Paul Krassner, the Beatles, and Bob Dylan. Like Leonard Cohen.

My senses were on high alert as I entered the large customs and immigration screening room. My fellow passengers formed lines for visitors, immigrants, and returning Canadians.

I waited in the visitors' line.

My greatest fear was being blocked from entering Canada.

I should have planned this better, I thought. I should have checked whether or not I'll be able to catch a plane to Sweden or France from the Montreal airport if Canada refuses to let me stay. I'd heard France and Sweden were the only other countries letting in people like me.

Everything I knew about escaping to Canada was hazy at best. All of it came from rumors from strangers.

Act normal, I told myself, hoping no one had noticed I'd exited America.

Maybe no one cares. Maybe I'm not on any list. Maybe the newly recommissioned prison camps around the US aren't for people like me.

I lifted my head and smiled pleasantly but not too pleasantly.

Look sharp but not too sharp. Don't stand out, I told myself.

I was twenty-two years old, nearly five-ten in height, slim, and athletic with blue eyes and fair skin. My hair was wavy and dark brown—long but not too long. My moustache was neatly trimmed.

I wondered if I should wear my glasses. They were gold wire rim specs like the ones John Lennon wore on the cover of the *Sgt. Pepper's* album. I bought the glasses at a fancy optometrist shop in Beverly Hills right after the album was released in June.

California seemed like a lifetime ago.

No glasses, I decided. I'm not wearing glasses in my passport photo.

My mother said I was the only one in the family who could pass. She meant that I looked more like a white American than anyone else in our family. I hoped that would help me clear immigration without any problems. I hadn't a clue what to expect.

Relax. Don't look suspicious. Act natural.

I moved up one place in line. Only one person was ahead of me.

I had two stories planned for the Canadian immigration officers. Both were more or less true.

"I am a writer," I intended to say, "working on a book. I thought I would stay in Montreal for a while and write." I could show them my portable typewriter and my manuscript in my duffle bag as proof.

My other story was more ambiguous: I'm coming to Montreal to take in the sights.

"I intend to travel around the country. I'm planning on doing some skating," I imagined saying.

The first part was true. As for skating, I packed an old pair of my father's skates in my bag on my last visit home. I hadn't been on skates in more than a decade. I hated skating. I felt foolish even having the skates with me. I wondered if they'd give me away.

The immigration officer began interviewing the man in front of me. I was next.

The Realist, an underground tabloid that circulated across the US, had recently published a story about the US government's plans to secretly reactivate the old internment camps used to imprison Japanese-American citizens during World War II. The camps were on standby, ready to be filled with every freak, peacenik, hippie, and protestor as soon as the US officially declared war on North Vietnam, which I kept hearing was imminent.

Once war is declared, my friends in the Los Angeles music and film industries had assured me, the government would be free to declare martial law and arrest anyone they pleased.

Stop thinking about the war.

Be a Zen Buddha, I told myself, not sure what that really meant.

Look happy but not too happy.

The screening officer signaled me with a wave of his hand.

He asked for identification. I handed him my passport. It was my first passport. I tried to look as confident as I did in the photo. My Uncle Sam, the second-most decorated war hero in our family, insisted I get a passport before I left the US. "War is all bullshit," he had been telling me since I was a kid.

"What brings you to Montreal?" the immigration officer asked me.

The war in Vietnam. The war on America's streets. I'm betting my country is on the wrong side of history. You can't fight a war on spaceship earth without shooting yourself in the foot.

"I was here two years ago on a short visit," I said. "I promised I'd come back."

"Where are you staying?"

"A friend of my uncle's. Crescent Street. Downtown." I gave the officer the name of my uncle's friend, hoping I was pronouncing it right.

The officer wrote something down, looked up, smiled, and told me, "Welcome to Canada. Have a nice visit."

He returned my passport and waved me through. It was that simple. No snarly guard dogs. No barbed wire. No face-slapping interrogators in a dank basement.

I've done it, I congratulated myself, standing outside the terminal and waiting for the shuttle bus to take me downtown. I have successfully left the US and crossed into Canada.

I breathed a sigh of relief, the first since flying out of La Guardia earlier in the day.

✷ ✷ ✷

Leaving the US turned out to be almost as simple as changing channels on a television set. Earlier I was in the US. An hour later, I was in a different country.

I felt good. I didn't have to tell any lies to get in. More important, I'd bought myself a little breathing room before I had to decide what to do next.

For the past three weeks, my only plan had been totally focused on getting out of the US, getting beyond the state of undeclared war, and starting life over. I had only a vague idea of what I would do once I got to Montreal. How hard could it be? Get working papers. Get a writing job. Find a place to live. Figure out the meaning of life.

The air in Montreal was colder and damper than New York. Near freezing. I wasn't sure what to expect from a Canadian winter.

I was wearing the only winter clothes I could find at my parents' house in rural New Jersey that still fit me—an old, dark-brown jacket made of horsehide and manufactured by my father as a prototype for soldiers during the Korean War, a pair of sheepskin gloves from my father's last glove factory, and a scarf smelling of mothballs that my mother had stored in one of the closets where she kept clothes she bought on sale. I tried to refuse the scarf. "Don't be a wise guy. You'll need this," she insisted.

The scarf came from the same closet where she kept my late grandfather's old neckties. "Grandpa lived in Glace Bay, Nova Scotia, Canada for a short time when he was a boy," she said. "The winters are brutal up there." I wanted to ask her more about Grandpa, Canada, and winter. I didn't have time.

The airport shuttle bus into Montreal traveled along the highway through the suburbs and then along the waterfront past massive sugar and grain silos before making a beeline for the gleaming new skyscrapers at the center of downtown.

This is the place, I told myself. The future.

Expo '67—some said the greatest World's Fair ever—had been in the news throughout the Summer of Love. The fair closed twelve days before I arrived. I was hoping some of the magic would still be there.

I breathed easy, reassuring myself I had made the right decision to leave the US. I was high on being in a new city and in a new country where I could erase the past and reinvent myself.

I'm in Canada, I kept reminding myself. I felt as happy as anyone on earth.

I was sure the worst of my new venture was over. I never suspected for a moment that over the next three days, I would fall in love, sleep on a cold floor, and discover I had made a terrible mistake crossing the border.

CHAPTER 2

I FELL QUICKLY in love with Katie.

After a quick stop at the apartment of my uncle's acquaintance on Crescent Street to drop off my duffle bag, I headed on foot straight to the campus of McGill University a half-dozen blocks away.

As soon as I reached the gates of the university, I saw a crowd of about two hundred students, a couple of dozen police, and a half-dozen police vehicles gathered in front of one of the imposing stone buildings on the other side of the grassy commons.

Looking like a student, I was certain I could blend in as I headed up the driveway. I told myself that if the demonstration turned violent I'd take off in a hurry.

By the time I reached the crowd, I realized the city police were hauling protesters out of the building, letting them go on the sidewalk in front, and barring the doors to anyone trying to return.

I scanned the crowd for a friendly face. A beautiful young woman standing near the front of the building caught me looking her way and smiled. She turned her eyes toward the doorway again as the crowd jeered at two brawny cops who appeared on the building's threshold, dragging the latest long-haired, skinny freak outdoors and letting him go on the driveway like they were removing pesky kittens from the building.

A tall guy with glasses and a moustache turned to the pretty woman and said something. She responded, then looked my way again.

I headed toward them and asked, "I'm new here. What's going on?"

The tall guy said, "The last student demonstrators are being evicted from the administration building."

The curious eyes of the woman peeked out from under her wool cap and seemed to be studying me intently. She reminded me a little bit of Jennifer.

"What are they protesting?" I asked both of them.

"Free speech. The administration kicked three of the staffers off the school paper, *The McGill Daily*, for publishing an article they found offensive," the fellow explained.

The *Daily* staff claimed they had the right to print anything they wanted. The article in dispute was a reprint of a satire written earlier in the year in *The Realist*. I was familiar with the article. It had been written by Paul Krassner, the most famous writer I knew besides the poet Allen Ginsberg. Paul Krassner was the founder, publisher, and editor of *The Realist*. He had written a scathing satire in the spring of 1967 on a recently published biography of President Kennedy. Krassner's satire was written in part to vilify President Johnson whom Krassner hated—he felt Johnson was responsible for escalating the Vietnam War. [1][2]

I had Krassner's phone number scribbled in the address book in my pocket. His number was one of my prized links with my past.

The pretty woman took a step closer and said, "You're one of the American soldiers, coming here because of the war."

I didn't think I stood out. I wasn't sure I wanted to. "What makes you think I'm American?"

"Your accent."

I didn't know I had one.

She introduced herself as Katie. "I've been hearing about soldiers coming to Canada because of the war for the past year. You're the first one I've met." Her friend was Greg. They had skipped class to watch the demonstration. They were both undergrads at McGill.

I wasn't yet sure what I was. "I'm not a soldier. I'm against the war. I decided to leave before I was called up."

In a political sense, I was (take your pick):

...one of the first war resisters to go to Canada,

...a draft dodger,

...a traitor to my country in time of war,

...a coward,

...an American exile in a foreign country,

...a fugitive from the FBI.

"You're all soldiers to me," Katie insisted. The sparkle in her eyes lit up her face.

A gust of cold wind blew through the commons, making everyone instinctively turn to block it. Katie brushed a long strand of light brown hair away from her eyes. Montreal was growing colder by the minute as the sun sank lower in the sky.

Two tall, broad-shouldered cops dragged another short, scrawny, long-haired student from the building and let him go on the driveway, blocking his feeble attempt to return inside. An older man in a suit—a professor or administrator—came to the doorway and announced: "It's over. You can all go home." He stepped inside again and closed the door. The police walked to their cars and drove off without arresting anyone.

Protests in Canada seemed far more civil than they had in the US.

The crowd began to wander away in all directions. Greg headed off by himself to meet someone. Katie said she had time for a coffee before heading home.

As we headed toward a bar she thought I would like, Katie told me she was studying English and theater. She had already starred in a short film made by a young filmmaker at the National Film Board.

I told her about my book and the film I wanted to write.

She took me to Le Bistro, a wonderfully noisy French pub on Mountain Street a few blocks away.

She was too young to drink legally, but no one seemed to mind. We drank Dubonnet, a French wine-based aperitif, and coffee, and Perrier—French club soda as far as I could tell—all new to me. The cigarettes were different, too—Players, Rothmans, Gauloises, Gitanes.

A well-dressed, clean-shaven, older man in a cashmere coat nodded to Katie as he made his way through the crowd toward the rear of the pub.

Once he passed by, she asked, "Do you know who that is?"

"No."

"Robert Hershorn, the film producer. One of Leonard Cohen's best friends. Leonard comes here all the time when he's in town. You know who Leonard Cohen is, don't you?" she asked with a teasing smile and narrowed eyes.

"Yes," I said. She was surprised when I told her I not only knew who Leonard Cohen was but that he had written the Judy Collins hit song, "Suzanne." More surprising to her, I had seen the documentary about him, *Ladies and Gentlemen, Mr. Leonard Cohen.*

Le Bistro and Hershorn, she told me, had been in the film.

Her favorite Dylan album was *Bringing It All Back Home.* "I took my first acid trip while listening to it," she said.

We quizzed each other on authors, filmmakers, and musicians.

"Yes, yes, and yes," she laughed when I asked her if she had heard of the Doors, Jefferson Airplane, and Big Brother and The Holding Company.

She made me feel at home and homesick. My face must have given me away. She reached across the table and took my hand. "It's really bad in the States, isn't it?"

I nodded and changed the subject. I had to get used to the idea that I might never be able to return to the US for the rest of my life. I half-listened to the stories she told me of her sisters and friends taking off and traveling across the country and to Europe, living on nothing, stopping where they pleased, and smoking hashish. She told me she wanted to take a camera, travel somewhere, and shoot a movie along the way. "Did you know that cinéma vérité was invented in Montreal at the film board?" She dazzled me with the names of local filmmakers who had made the first cinéma vérité movies at the film board and then gone to France and introduced their methods to some of the top French directors.

I fell in love with the sexiness in her voice and the way she threw her head back and laughed with great vitality. I told her about California, the Watts Riots, Allen Ginsberg, Edie Sedgwick, the first Love-In, South Central, Sunset Strip, East LA, Venice Beach, Malibu, San Francisco, and Big Sur. She told me about skiing in the Laurentians during the winter and canoeing on one of the lakes far to the north during the summer.

I fell in love because I needed to be in love. By stupid dumb luck, I had fallen right into it hours after arriving. Montreal, I thought, was turning out just as I wanted it to.

We kissed, held hands, and held tightly onto each other as we walked against the cold winds on our way to the train station.

At the station in the basement of the Queen Elizabeth Hotel, we hugged and kissed and promised to meet again the next day for lunch.

Then, Katie was gone. Her train took her underground a few miles north through a tunnel in the mountain to the other side of the city.

Everything will be okay, I told myself as I walked the dozen blocks from the station back to the apartment of my uncle's acquaintance on Crescent Street.

Montreal is sexy, alive, away from the war, I thought. I wondered what it must have been like for Hemingway and Fitzgerald on their first day in Paris in the 1920s.

All I needed to do was officially declare my intentions to stay.

Everything seemed so simple and perfect.

It wasn't, of course.

CHAPTER 3

EMILE AND I read each other completely wrong at the beginning.

Emile Pirro, a graphic artist, and my Uncle Sam, a well-known New York agent for photographers and artists, had done business together over the phone and by mail, but they had never met.

My uncle had arranged some design work for Emile during the height of Expo '67. When I told my uncle I was leaving the country and heading to Montreal, he called Emile and asked if he could put me up for a few days until I got my bearings. Emile said yes without hesitating.

I expected Emile to be well-off like my uncle and the others I'd met in advertising in New York and Los Angeles. In New York, I had worked a few times as an assistant on shoots for an airline and a car manufacturer for well-known photographer George Elliott. In LA, I had worked on a shoot for the equally renowned Don Ornitz. The grunt work on the photo shoots paid more in a day than I normally made in two weeks at my usual minimum wage jobs. I was convinced that everyone in advertising was rich. So, when I first arrived, I wasn't surprised to find Emile living in a tony neighborhood of turn-of-the-century stone and brick townhouses on Crescent Street close to the center of downtown. An upscale dress shop was located on the ground floor of his building.

Emile's studio and residence were located up a long, steep flight of stairs on the second floor.

When I first arrived from the airport, Emile had greeted me at the door with an ear-to-ear grin. He was in his late thirties or early forties, small, and pudgy with pasty skin, and dark, curly ringlets of hair down to his shoulders. He was dressed in dark slacks and a white shirt, sleeves rolled up to his elbows. From the hallway, I caught a glimpse of a cluttered graphics studio off to my right.

"Sorry I can't spend more time with you right now. I'm finishing off a rush job," Emile apologized. "You can leave your things here." He took my duffle bag and stuffed it into the hall closet. "We'll have dinner together later if you don't have other plans."

In the doorway, down the hall in the other direction, stood an ancient, tiny, white-haired lady with thick glasses that magnified her eyes to twice their size. An even older-looking Spaniel stood beside her.

"Dinner sounds great," I told him. We set a time, and I went straight to McGill a half-dozen blocks away and met Katie.

After saying goodbye to Katie at the train station and starting back to Emile's, I felt proud of myself that I already knew north, south, east, and west, and a half-dozen streets west of the train station. I made it back without asking anyone for directions.

Emile and his girlfriend, Mona, were both dressed and ready to go to dinner when I returned. She appeared to me to be in her thirties with a round, pleasant face, straight, dark hair cut short, and pale skin. She was wearing a tight-fitting black skirt and a lacy blouse. Emile was wearing a white shirt open a couple of buttons at the top, dark pants, and shiny red patent leather loafers, which he was very proud of.

The old woman, who I had seen earlier, came to the door to say goodbye. Emile introduced me to his mother and her half-blind dog. "You'll be safe here," she told me in warm, heavily French-accented English.

I learned on the way to the restaurant that Emile lived in his apartment with his mother and stayed some nights with Mona in the apartment building we passed on the way to dinner. Mona worked as a secretary and sometimes model for a dress manufacturer.

They took me to a lively French restaurant on St. Catherine Street. It was on the second floor overlooking the busy street below. The restaurant was crowded with well-dressed people. The prices on the menu were extravagant. Emile suggested the frogs' legs as an appetizer and the steak and frites as my main dish. Of course, I let Emile order the wine. I knew nothing about fine vintages.

By the time we had finished dessert, I learned Emile was the son of a French-Canadian mother and a recently deceased Italian immigrant mason father, who had lost a leg building the great stone Canada Life Assurance Company edifice in the center of the city during the Depression. Emile had a collection of comic books dating to the 1930s, and the falloff in business as Expo wound down was so severe he was a couple of months behind in his rent.

"I'm not broke," he insisted. "I have plenty of work. Nobody's paying on time."

By the time the check came, I realized he thought I was some rich kid who'd been sent by his parents to get out of the cold.

The check was more than it cost me to live for a month in LA. I had been scraping by on nothing for years. My parents were barely holding their own heads above the poverty line. I didn't have the heart to tell him then. I paid the check and gave the waiter a generous tip. It felt good to pretend for a moment that I did come from money.

After we dropped Mona off at her place and returned to Emile's, he gave me a tour of the front half of his flat. He operated his one-man studio out of the large, front room. Off of it was a small, poorly heated storage room with boxes and no furniture and enough space on the floor for me to sleep—my room until I found my own place.

The bathroom consisted of two rooms—the tub in one, the sink and a toilet in the other. "Common design in France and parts of Quebec," he explained, "and don't be fooled by the two 'Cs' on the hot and cold knobs of the sink. On the right, it's 'C' for cold. On the left, it's 'C' for *chaud*, French for hot. At least, that's what the plumber told me." He laughed and shook his head as if to say crazy things like that were common in Quebec.

When he discovered I hadn't brought a sleeping bag, he located a threadbare blanket from a closet in back. "It's all I have," he apologized.

I told him I had slept on the ground before. "I was in the Scouts as a kid."

I also told him I wasn't much better off than him. I certainly wasn't rich.

"I shouldn't have taken you to that restaurant," he said sheepishly.

"Don't worry. I'll be fine, Emile. The dinner will give me something special to remember about my first night in Canada."

The floor, even with my clothes on, was like ice. The blanket barely made a difference. I tried not to notice. For the moment, I was safe. I fell asleep thinking about Katie.

CHAPTER 4

KATIE AND I spent the next two days together. She took me to the top of Mount Royal—the mountain in the middle of the Island of Montreal—for a grand look at the city and the St. Lawrence River. She showed me another way down the mountain through the McGill campus. Admittedly obsessed with Leonard Cohen, she took me to the Main—the lower St. Lawrence Boulevard, the north-south street that divided the east and west sides of the city—and showed me the pool halls with their hotdog stands and arcade games in front and pool tables in back surrounded by seedy old men. Leonard Cohen's Montreal, she called it.

"He made it out of here onto the world stage," Katie said, explaining her fixation on Leonard Cohen. English Montreal was a tiny village inside a much larger French city. Cohen had broken out, gone to New York, and become an international celebrity. He was the envy of every poet, writer, and musician in the city, including every Francophone who dreamed of becoming a star on the international stage. No one else represented Montreal's youth more than he did. I laughed to myself when I realized he had broken out, seemingly, just as I had broken in.

In Old Montreal—*Vieux-Montréal*—she showed me the Notre-Dame-de-Bon-Secours Chapel—the old Sailors' Church, and pointed to the building on the opposite side of the street where Suzanne had lived and served Leonard Cohen tea and exotic oranges from Asia.

"And hashish," Katie said. No one smoked grass. It was too bulky to smuggle in large quantities from Mexico or elsewhere in Latin America. The hashish came by boat and plane from Morocco, Lebanon, and India.

Her friend, Greg was leaving in the spring to live in India. He promised to send her hashish by mail.

"If you can't stay in Canada, take me with you," she insisted, clinging to me tighter as we braved the cold winds off the harbor. I wondered if I would have the nerve to start over in another country if I had to leave Canada.

On the return walk to the center of town she showed me a new steakhouse on one of the main streets, part of a small chain of local restaurants her father was promoting on the stock market.

On Monday morning, I left Emile's feeling determined to face my fate as I hiked several blocks west to the address I'd written down before I left California.

The address came from a couple of morose revolutionaries passing out anti-war literature at UCLA, where I had briefly attended grad school. The revolutionaries said they had heard of a handful of Americans who had gone to Canada to protest the draft and the war. They didn't know any personally.

I had never met or heard of anyone who had gone to Canada to resist the draft. No one in any of my circles of friends knew anyone who made the trek across the border to live in Canada.

The UCLA revolutionaries said they had heard that the fastest and best way to apply for immigrant status in Canada was to arrive as a visitor and then apply from inside the country.

"If the Canadians don't find anything wrong with you, they'll take your application and begin processing it, and they'll give you a temporary work permit right away." It sounded like a good plan. As a tourist, I could look around first before deciding to actually apply to immigrate.

Falling in love with Katie hours after I arrived made it easy for me to decide to stay. I didn't need two or three weeks to make up my mind.

I found the address I was looking for, rang the buzzer, and told myself, here goes.

The clean-shaven guy in a striped shirt, chinos, and short hair let me in and told me bluntly, "You received outdated advice. The situation has changed. Canada is no longer granting instant work permits to tourists already in the country. That stopped a few months ago. Now, the only way to get temporary working papers immediately is to apply at a border crossing or at the immigration desk in an airport when you first arrive. You should have said you wanted to immigrate when you came through the airport."

Major bummer, I thought. The information stunned me. I had made a colossal error at the airport.

I wasn't home free at all but still in limbo.

CHAPTER 5

THE ONLY GOOD news was that I could *still* apply to become a legal immigrant from inside the country, but it might take six months before I got a work permit. I wasn't sure how long my money would last.

I had survived on my own in Los Angeles for four years on a half-dozen part-time odd jobs: washing dishes at a frat house, hauling boxes for the library, recreational counselor for the Boy's Club in Boyle Heights, butcher's assistant in a country store in the Hollywood Hills, textbook writer for one my professors, and occasional assistant and jack-of-all-trades for photographers on both coasts. Part of the money I had on me came from my last American job—driving cars for a photographer shooting a print campaign for a new line of automobiles on an abandoned estate on Long Island—just days before I hopped a plane out of the country.

The prices of everything in Canada seemed higher than in California, but I thought if I was careful, I might be able hold out without working for several months.

One thing for certain, I wasn't going back.

I reckoned my notice of withdrawal from UCLA grad school had arrived at my draft board by then. The board would immediately reclassify me "1-A," making me instantly eligible for the draft.

I had no idea how long it would take for the draft board to order me to report for my physical, but I suspected it would be soon. Draft boards across the country were nabbing everyone who didn't have a student deferment or exemption of some kind.

I was also wary of flying back to the US, fearing my name might already be on a watch list at the US border.

Later that morning, I went to the Canadian immigration offices. The clerk at the information desk told me, "The process could take six months with no guarantee you'll be accepted."

If I returned to the US and refused to take the oath for the Army I could spend the next five years in a federal penitentiary.

Mentally, I couldn't go back. It had taken too much effort to psych myself into leaving in the first place. For an American like me, born and bred to believe I lived in the best country in the world, turning my back on the US government and its military machine was more difficult than breaking any of the Ten Commandments.

The only advice I was given when I filled out my application was: "Don't work illegally or you could risk being deported."

Montreal suddenly felt more like wartime Morocco in the Humphrey Bogart movie *Casablanca* than the Paris of F. Scott Fitzgerald or Hemingway. I was on shaky ground, stateless, and unsure what the long arm of the US government could legally and illegally do to me.

CHAPTER 6

BY TUESDAY, I witnessed my first snowfall in five years.

I hated to be cold. I hated being stateless, but for the moment, I was safe. The killing machine of the war had already brought death to nearly 18,000 US soldiers and hundreds of thousands of Vietnamese soldiers and civilians.

War had never been declared. It had just snuck up on us and turned into a full-blown conflict that was sucking the life out of the US. In the two and a half years since President Johnson had sent combat troops to fight in Vietnam, I hadn't heard a single convincing argument for why I should be willing to lay down my life there. I hadn't once felt threatened by the Viet Cong or North Vietnamese. I had no reason to want to kill anyone in Southeast Asia, or anywhere for that matter. Not one single friend, male or female, thought the war was a worthwhile cause. Most disturbing, we were destroying the very people we were supposed to be helping.

Worst-case scenario in my mind was that by sending more combat troops to Vietnam, we risked sucking in China and the USSR, both of which had nuclear weapons. I was the first generation to grow up with the possibility of a nuclear Armageddon. As a kid, I had been obsessed with the bomb. The last thing I wanted to do was hasten a nuclear firestorm.

The war is over, finished for me, I told myself. Stay strong.

★ ★ ★

The wait to see if my application would get a preliminary review put me in no-man's land. If my gamble didn't pay off, I hoped I'd still have enough money to buy a plane ticket to Sweden or France. Emile showed me on one of his maps two little islands off the east coast of Canada—St. Pierre and Miquelon—still owned by France. The islands were their last bit of their once-enormous empire of New France. He thought I might be able to go there.

"If I get any farther behind in my rent, I might go with you," he joked.

I was equally astonished when looking at Emile's map to see Montreal was hundreds of miles from the ocean. I had never looked at a map before emigrating. I just assumed that Montreal was on the coast, somewhere vaguely north of Boston and Maine.

Typical stupid American, I thought. I had to laugh to keep from crying.

To bolster my spirits while waiting, I found a furnished basement room on Aylmer Street between Sherbrooke and Milton, a few blocks east of the McGill campus. My place was about the size of a motel room—large enough for a shabby couch that flattened into a bed; a table for dining, writing, and sketching; a couple of chairs; a hotplate, sink, and very noisy refrigerator with a compressor that turned on and off day and night and kept me awake until I was too tired to hear it.

The snowfalls in Montreal were far worse than anything I'd experienced growing up in rural New Jersey. The snow didn't melt off in a few days but piled up on the streets as more fell on top. Tiny plows like miniature tanks scraped the sidewalks clean, leaving chest-high piles of dirty snow between the street and the sidewalk. My apartment never seemed to get warm.

I tried to work on my novel, but I could never make it past the first few chapters without wanting to tear it to shreds.

Be patient, I counseled myself. I had never been good at sitting still.

My mother forwarded a plain envelope to Emile's address. Inside was the notice from my draft board in New Jersey reclassifying me "1-A"—immediately eligible for the draft. I could expect my notice to report for my physical soon. Once I missed that, my file would be turned over to the FBI, if it hadn't already been.

The FBI. They were the people who hunted interstate murderers, kidnappers, Nazis, Communist spies, and organized crime figures. The idea of being a fugitive from the FBI was so horrific that I would have been utterly terrified if it didn't also feel so surreal.

None of what is going on could possibly be happening to me or to the world, I continued to tell myself. Half-defiant, half-scared, I reassured myself that no reality existed except what I made of it in my own mind. I had to learn to think differently if I was to survive in an alternate universe.

I felt ignorant not knowing much about Canada and its problems. Emile began educating me about the age-old divide between the English-speaking minorities and the French-speaking majority in Quebec. The rivalry had turned violent over the past four years.

A gang of young, mostly homegrown *Québécois* leftist revolutionaries had formed an underground separatist movement in 1963 called the Front de libération du Québec or FLQ. [3] "They want to drive English speakers out of the province and establish a French-speaking socialist state," Emile explained with a shrug. "The FLQ has been blowing up mailboxes and setting bombs off in front of government buildings associated with anything English. They've killed several people. The latest attack was a month ago." A bomb had been detonated at a 7Up bottling plant in Mount Royal during a strike only weeks before I arrived.

I wondered what the chances were of Quebec collapsing into civil war. I had witnessed the Watts Riots in Los Angeles firsthand two years earlier. The experience had sickened me and convinced me I wanted no part of war if I could help it.

I had no phone in my apartment, partly to save money and partly to make finding me more difficult. Only a few people even knew I had gone to Canada, and those few who wrote sent their letters to Emile's address on Crescent Street with only his company name on the envelope. My rare telephone calls to rural New Jersey were always from payphones on the street.

About once a week, my mother and I exchanged letters. She used her maiden name on her envelopes as part of our subterfuge.

"Now we are down to the real thing.... If I go back to the States," I wrote in a burst of bravado and fatalism, "I shall probably go to jail...."

I had toured jails with the Scouts as a kid, and more recently when I was studying psychology and sociology as an undergrad at the University of Southern California (USC). Nearly half of my closest friends had been busted at one time or another for pot and other psychedelics. Once, six friends had been caught in a raid just minutes after I had left a party. I had no romantic ideas about prison.

I kept finding little things about Montreal that were different. Everyone hugged as a greeting. The women kissed each other on both cheeks. No one wore shoes inside. Emile said everyone took off their shoes at the door even in summer.

My ratty apartment was Katie's first home away from home. She liked coming and going whenever she pleased. She liked interrupting my writing to cuddle with me on the couch under the blankets to keep warm. She wore a scent that reminded me of roses, of summertime.

She was passionate, sensual, and a virgin. She wanted to make love, but she was afraid that I would leave her.

She was right, of course. We couldn't talk about a future together.

I told her to take her time.

She wanted to be convinced her first time would be special. I had nothing to promise her.

After a few weeks, she told me about another student who was relentlessly pursuing her. She pretended it was a joke, but I could see it excited her.

"What should I do?"

"Whatever you like," I told her, knowing that nothing I said would matter. She wanted to be saved, enlightened, and transported to another world. I did, too. At the moment, I was going nowhere. I also knew I had already lost her.

"You don't care?"

"I care that you're happy," I said, telling her a half-truth. The other half was that I wanted to make love to her, to live with her naked beneath the covers, breathing in her scent, feeling her warmth and softness.

Katie started seeing her fellow student, but she still came to see me. She told me they were talking about quitting school, following Leonard

Cohen to Greece, and going to other exotic places. "You can come, too," she insisted.

"Maybe," I lied. I envied her freedom, her youth, and her carefree Canadian citizenship.

I tried to write away my discomfort and loss. For the first time, I was alone in Montreal, feeling stupid and useless more often than smart and clever.

I was willfully committing a crime. I had used love as a pill to get me through the first weeks. By the end of November, I was going through withdrawals, the shakes, the second-guessing, the double-checking, and worst of all, I found it impossible to write. I had run out of smart things to say.

I stared out the low basement window of my apartment, watching legs and boots of all kinds and sizes trampling through the snow along the sidewalk out front. Never any faces, just legs and boots. The top of the window cut off the rest. I thought of a strange arrangement I'd seen when the new Los Angeles County Museum of Art on Wilshire Boulevard opened a couple of years before. The artwork was composed of a newspaper with the headlines of Nazi General Rommel's defeat in the desert in North Africa by the Allied forces. Beneath the newspaper were a couple of pairs of old, worn, leather combat boots. I dragged everyone I knew to see what I renamed, "De-feeted."

★ ★ ★

If violence is a sickness, then war is the plague, I told myself.

★ ★ ★

I continued to look for ways to stretch my money. I bought the cheapest stew meat available at the grocery store. The meat was too tough to chew even after cooking it forever. I switched to hot dogs and drank gallons of instant coffee. I bought a large brick of margarine because it was cheaper than butter. I got a real shock when I opened the cardboard package. The Quebec margarine was a sickening lard-like white block. It came with a little gelatin capsule filled with yellow dye. To make the margarine yellow, I had to mix the dye and the margarine together in a bowl and knead it like dough until the white blob turned the color of butter. Emile told me the dairy farmers had pushed a bill through the Quebec legislature banning pre-dyed yellow margarine from the store shelves. Next time, I bought regular butter.

☆ ☆ ☆

One of the most disturbing letters I received came from a friend, Michael, a TV director in New York. Michael was in his early thirties, married, and living a successful life in Manhattan. He wrote that he was terrified by recent events in the US. He was an officer in the Army Reserve and had been mobilized. He wrote: "I just heard from a reliable friend—an engineer, who has just come back from Vietnam where he was designing and building prisons. He said the US is already secretly at war with the Chinese. He had personally seen captured Chinese POWs in the camps over there."

☆ ☆ ☆

I opened a bank account and was pleased to find that the exchange rate added an extra seven percent to my anti-war chest. I kept my passport, address book, and a few hundred dollars in cash and travelers' checks on me at all times in case I had to leave quickly.

I spent a lot of time alone, reading, trying to write, and going to countless old movies in shabby, second-run theaters with floors so sticky they threatened to pull the soles off my boots.

With no radio or television, I tried to keep up with the news by buying a French-English dictionary and reading the French newspapers. Translating was difficult for me, and in one letter to my friend, Sparky, at UC Berkeley, I wrote that, "I am not sure if Greece and Turkey are, will be, or have been at war."

Any sense of my own importance continued to fade. I found myself struggling each day to justify my life. The headiness of my big escape from the US had worn off, leaving me ragged, wondering what would come next.

I haven't killed anyone, I kept telling myself.

I questioned whether I was against all war or just this war. In this war, I was betting the US was on the wrong side of history. I felt I had a moral obligation to prevent nationalism from blinding me. Wasn't blind nationalism what we had blamed ordinary German and Japanese soldiers for in the Second World War?

If I refuse to be part of the war, if I remove one single person from war, I am doing some good, I rationalized. If I don't and I have the chance, then I *am* a coward.

I replayed in my mind what Aldous Huxley once wrote about war: "What is absurd and monstrous about war is that men who have no personal quarrel should be trained to murder one another in cold blood."

And yet, if I had let myself be drafted and gone to Vietnam, I had no doubt I would shoot back, kill, and avoid being killed. Scare me enough, brainwash me enough, corner me completely, and I could be a killer. I hated that part of me.

I started a new novel about a young freak, oddball, outsider, who travels from New York to Los Angeles and back again as his country lunges into war on the wrong side. My character thinks it's all crazy. He finally goes to Montreal, looking for meaning, running from meaning, and trying to understand what meaning *means* while all the time feeling slightly detached—more like someone watching himself move through life rather than living it.

My new novel sounded too much like the life I was leading. I threw it out.

I thought about drugs and stayed away from drugs. I was determined to avoid deportation.

★ ★ ★

My mother wrote that my Aunt Mollie died. Aunt Mollie was my father's oldest sister—an overweight, odd duck who never married but had memorized everyone's telephone number and birthday. She had acted as a surrogate mother for her siblings—including my then-nine-year-old father—after their mother died. Aunt Mollie had lived on handouts all her life and died at sixty-one from cancer. She was the first of my aunts and uncles on either side to die. I couldn't go to her funeral.

★ ★ ★

It felt strange living in a place where no one knew it was American Thanksgiving.

★ ★ ★

The secret of my escape to Canada soon leaked out among my extended family. Great Uncle Lew, a childhood friend of *Time* magazine founder, Henry Luce; an amateur boxer in the US Navy, and veteran of World War

I, was furious, because I hadn't gone into the Navy as he had suggested. He was certain that I was ruining my life. He was even more upset because I'd lied to him about what I was doing when I said goodbye. I told him I'd quit school to travel the world like his favorite author, Jack London, so I could find something worth writing about.

My Uncle Joe, who had served overseas during World War II running one of the US Army officers' clubs in Italy—thought I should accept the situation in the US, join the Army, and hope the war would be over by then.

What makes him think the war will be over, I wondered. I was dead certain that the US would soon put ground troops into North Vietnam. The number of Americans in Vietnam had gone from twenty-three thousand, when the first US combat soldiers had landed in South Vietnam early in 1965, to hundreds of thousands in the last months of 1967. How many of us would they need to draft to put a million troops on the ground in Vietnam?

"I wonder if you need a passport to get into Atlantis," I wrote home.

★ ★ ★

Katie stopped by late one night. She still hadn't decided who should be the first one to sleep with her. She said she loved me more than her new boyfriend. She said she would see me on the weekend.

I wasn't surprised when she didn't show.

★ ★ ★

I bought some small tubes of acrylic paint, brushes, and pre-stretched canvases, and began to paint.

"Light touches of snow, then rain, then snow, then rain, again," I wrote to my mother. "The weather amuses me."

I saw signs of hope that the anti-war movement in the US wasn't just a children's crusade made up of dreamers, freaks, and clowns under the age of thirty.

Secretary of Defense Robert McNamara called the bombing of North Vietnam ineffective. He resigned his post after clashing with President Johnson over the direction of the war. Eugene McCarthy, a barely known US Senator from Minnesota and an anti-war Democrat, decided to run for President challenging President Johnson, a fellow Democrat.

But the war camp was still in ascent. General Westmoreland told *Time* magazine, "I hope [the Viet Cong] try something because we are looking for a fight." He would soon get what he longed for—the Tet offensive.

I fought constantly against thinking what might have been if the US wasn't at war.

Troop levels in Vietnam reached 463,000 by the end of the year with nearly 20,000 American service personnel already killed, more than half of those in 1967, with inevitably more to come.

Unbeknownst to the public at the time, North Vietnam rejected President Johnson's secret appeal to end the war.

On the last day of mail delivery before the New Year, I received a letter telling me to report to the local Canadian immigration office in two weeks.

CHAPTER 7

I SPENT THE first days of the New Year in my room painting and writing. The temperature plunged to twenty below zero Fahrenheit, then twenty-five below. My room always felt cold.

✷ ✷ ✷

On the tenth day of the New Year, two months after I arrived in Montreal, I walked down the hill in the subzero temperature promising myself that if the Canadian immigration authorities accepted my application for processing, I would invest in a hat.

The receptionist was cheery. She made me feel like she was happy to see me, something I'd never experienced in government offices in the US.

I expected the friendliness to end at the receptionist desk. After a short wait, I was brought to an immigration officer. He greeted me with a big smile and a handshake.

"Nice to see you," he said.

I tried to stay wary but the friendliness was disarming. He was only a few years older than me, French Canadian, fluently bilingual, upbeat, and personable. The good cop without the bad cop anywhere in sight. He double-checked the answers on my application and gave me—I think—more points for my smattering of French than I deserved. My bachelor's degree in psychology from USC gave me more points. Then, he asked me if I had left the US because of the draft.

When I hesitated he said, "Don't worry. I'm not writing this down. You don't have to tell me. I'm just curious. Canada wants educated people like you." He just seemed to want to chat.

"I left before I was drafted." I said, not sure what my status was in the US at that moment.

"We have other Americans like you here, and also French, Greeks, and men from other countries escaping their military and wars."

He told me he thought several thousand American men of draft age might already be in Canada, but that included students who had deferments and others who had medical and other exemptions. No one knew the true figures.

The good news was that my application had been accepted for processing. I scored more than enough points to qualify for landed immigrant status even without much French. I needed to pass a medical exam. Everything would be reviewed in Ottawa. That could take another three or four months. I still couldn't work for those months, but I had crossed the first hurdle. I had a chance to join a new country, erase my past, and start fresh.

CHAPTER 8

I BOUGHT A wool tuque—a knitted wool cap—from Eaton's department store. I purchased a cheap, bright red Taiwanese radio from Payettes. I picked up a roll of canvas and an armload of stretcher bars from the art supply shop on Sherbrooke Street near l'École des beaux-arts. I felt settled enough to buy large jars of acrylics instead of small tubes.

My notice from my draft board to report for my physical arrived at my parents' house in New Jersey the same day I passed my preliminary interview at the immigration office. The letter ordered me to report for my Army physical on January 23, three months after I had officially dropped out of UCLA grad school.

★ ★ ★

A week later, my mother wrote that Billy was in the military brig at Fort Dix, New Jersey.

I was shocked. Billy was the son of close family friends who lived in Newark. He was a tough but likable kid who had been a high school football star and had become something of a local hero because he had a reputation for defending some of the local weaker kids.

I saw him a few times a year. A year older than me and taller and tougher, we wandered around his neighborhood and joked about ways we could hijack the local ice cream truck. When he came to our house in the country, I showed him my .22 and took him into the back fields where he saw for the first time a hunter shoot a pheasant out of the air with a shotgun. Our families went together one Christmas to Rockefeller Center. We shook hands with Zero Mostel and got his autograph. Neither of us had any idea who Zero Mostel was.

Now, Billy was in a military jail. He had tried junior college for a short time but had dropped out. I'd heard he had been drafted the previous year when I was still at USC on the other side of the country. During the intervening months, I heard from my mother he had been through basic training and was home waiting for orders. In actual fact, when Billy found out he was being sent to Vietnam after basic training, he simply walked off the base and went underground. He had been Away without Leave (AWOL) for almost a year. He turned himself in just days before being declared a deserter. He was waiting to stand trial.

I wrote to my mother that Billy's stance made me feel stronger and more defiant. "How come so many of us are willing to go to jail or leave the country? There's something rotten in the States."

Why weren't Canada, Great Britain, France, and the Scandinavian countries, and most of the rest of the world at war in Vietnam? Was Canada too weak to defend world liberty, or was it possible that world liberty wasn't in jeopardy?

And where was the UN? If the civil war in Vietnam between two halves of an artificially divided country was such a threat to the rest of humanity then the UN should send in troops. [4] By this time, I was tired of hiding. I sent my draft board a letter, giving them Emile's address and instructing them to write me there—no long letter of explanation, no apology, no declaration of my political beliefs, no anti-war poems, just a line informing them that if they wanted to correspond with me they should use my new Canadian address.

★ ★ ★

South Vietnam boiled over into hell on January 31, 1968. The Viet Cong and the North Vietnamese Army launched all-out attacks against military and civilian command-and-control centers of the US and South Vietnamese. The objective was to foster a general popular uprising among the South Vietnamese public against the South Vietnamese military and the US. It was called the Tet Offensive—after the Vietnamese Tet New Year celebration. It was the largest military operation to that point during the war and included more than 300,000 North Vietnam and Viet Cong combat and support troops. Total Allied casualties during the January-February action were more than 45,000, including more than 9,000 deaths. The Viet Cong and North Vietnamese Army suffered an estimated 17,000 killed and 20,000 wounded in what was phase one of a three-phase offensive that would continue later in the spring and summer.

Although the North Vietnamese failed in their strategic objective to get the South Vietnamese people to revolt against the South Vietnamese government, their attacks helped increase anti-war sentiment among the American public.

The death and destruction on both sides made me sick. I did not want either side to win. I wanted them both to stop.

My Uncle Sam wrote to tell me to expect a large exodus out of the US by people opposed to the war, not just draft-aged people but ordinary citizens against the US involvement in Vietnam, and soon.

"Keep cots and warm soup ready for us," he advised me half-seriously.

I wondered if our letters were being monitored.

CHAPTER 9

I MET OSKAR the poster king through Andrew at the end of February.

I still didn't have working papers, and my money was running out. So, I had started knocking on doors, trying to line up work for March or April when I was hoping my work permit would come through. I knew I'd need something soon to avoid ending up on the street.

I was out one afternoon checking on a future job prospect at the library when I stumbled on a man struggling to open the door of an office building on one of the windiest days of the winter.

When I got close, I realized he was having trouble breathing. He was in such bad shape that I had to help him inside. We stopped while he caught his breath. When he was finally able to talk, he told me his name was Andrew. He worked as an account executive in one of the big advertising agencies. He had just returned to Montreal from Toronto where he had had some polyps removed from his lungs. When I told him I was a writer looking for work in the coming months he said, "Forget the advertising business. They're still laying off people, but if you're looking for something to fill in until things pick up, you should speak to my partner, Oskar. He might need someone."

He handed me his card before disappearing into the elevator to meet a client.

The card said: International Art and Design.

The name sounded impressive. The address was only a few blocks away on Mountain Street.

The address turned out to be only a couple of doors north of Le Bistro over a chic fashion boutique on the ground floor.

My mood brightened as I climbed the stairs. I could hear the latest Beatles' album, *Magical Mystery Tour,* playing softly at the top.

What I found as I stepped through the door was totally unexpected.

The walls from floor to ceiling of the first room were covered with the most posters I had seen anywhere. Through an archway that led to a second large room at the front of the suite, I saw still more posters covering every inch of the walls.

It's some kind of gallery, I thought.

Except for a clean-shaven man talking on a telephone in a small office off to one side, the place was empty. As soon as the fellow saw me, he put down the phone and came forward to greet me with a broad smile and an outstretched hand. He was about my age with angular features, a strong chin, and sharp nose. He was dressed casually in an open-necked white shirt and slacks. His hair was straight, brown, and just long enough to pass for hip or straight.

The man greeted me in French. I replied in French and switched to English to tell him I was looking for Oskar.

"I'm Oskar," he replied cheerfully in English with a slight accent that I couldn't quite identify.

I told him I had just met Andrew and was looking for work once my papers came through.

"I'm a writer," I explained. "I'm not sure if you're looking for someone like me."

"I'm a landscape architect by training and profession," he said with an easy laugh. "A year ago, I never imagined I would be in the poster business. Let me show you around."

Oskar was Swiss and was fluent in German, English, and French. He could get by in Spanish and Italian. He was a couple of years older than me and had completed his military service after university. I was the first war resister he had met since arriving in Canada during Expo the previous year.

"I would have done the same thing as you if anyone had tried to send me to Vietnam," he said. "The majority of the Vietnamese people don't want foreigners there telling them how to run their country."

The poster craze was just taking off internationally. Some thought it was just a passing fad, but it seemed to be growing in popularity. Oskar had caught the first wave. He had come to Canada during the early summer at the beginning of the World's Fair on the first leg of a trip around the world. Before hopping the boat from Amsterdam to Montreal, he discovered a printer in Amsterdam with stacks of high-grade Henri de Toulouse-Lautrec posters. On a whim, Oskar bought a bunch, wrapped them in plastic, and carried them across the Atlantic intending to sell them on the downtown streets of Montreal to earn enough money to pay for a few days in the city before moving on.

"After the first day, I wandered into a couple of the department stores and realized no one was selling posters."

Except for a few samples, he sold all the posters he had, ordered more, and began to take orders from department stores, bookstores, record stores, and the handful of struggling head shops in town. Within a few months, he had made deals with a dozen different sources of posters from major American companies to the small, boutique printers and artists turning out posters in Montreal and Europe.

"What do you think?" he asked.

A quarter of the posters were the black-and-white celebrity posters that were just becoming popular in Los Angeles in my last years there. They ranged from Elvis, Humphrey Bogart, W.C. Fields, and Marilyn Monroe to Allen Ginsberg wearing an American flag top hat, Fidel Castro in a Russian hat with ear flaps, Bob Dylan with his hand over his eyes, and several polychrome and black-and-white posters of Che Guevara.

A corner of the front room was devoted to psychedelic posters. The four solarized portraits of the Beatles that Richard Avedon had shot earlier in the year adorned a portion of another wall. Beside it were fine English prints of Aubrey Beardsley's drawings.

In the room overlooking the street were wild, colorful posters in French and other languages I couldn't read.

"Amazing," I said. "So this is your showroom?"

"Showroom and retail shop—my first attempt at selling directly to the public."

The store had been open only a few days. Before that he had operated entirely out of the apartment he shared with Andrew not far from downtown.

"I haven't had much success so far attracting people upstairs to the shop. You're the first person who's been here all day. Any ideas what I should do?"

Flattered to be asked, I tried to think of a way to make myself useful. "If it was my place, I'd print flyers and hand them out on the street. I'd keep wholesaling the cheap celebrity and psychedelic posters to the other stores but get rid of them here. Turn this into a fine arts gallery for unusual posters."

"Maybe you should be in the poster business," he said grinning.

Over the next few weeks while I waited for my work permit, I threw myself into working for free, selling posters just to see what the business was like. Retailing and wholesaling posters was the best and only job prospect I had. I figured learning about the business world in general couldn't hurt.

Oskar said if I worked out and the business could take in enough, we could talk about what I would make once I officially was able to work.

I was flattered that Oskar thought I was clever. Together, we designed a black-and-white broadsheet advertising the shop. He printed a few hundred on newsprint. Each day one of us spent an hour or more handing out flyers on the sidewalk in the freezing wind while the other manned the store. We talked to everyone we could stop on the street—university students from McGill, Loyola, and Sir George; executives from nearby advertising companies; TV personalities and newspaper reporters who hung out at Le Bistro; and leisure shoppers visiting the nearby boutiques. Pretty soon, word got out that Oskar had the coolest poster shop in town.

But even with the store and the wholesale business Oskar was still barely breaking even. The profit on each poster was miniscule.

"It'll get better," Oskar insisted. "When I first arrived I was only able to afford a room. Now, I share a three-bedroom apartment with Andrew and I have a shop."

Oskar's enthusiasm and unbridled energy were infectious. I followed along, volunteering for everything. We took turns delivering weekly shipments of posters and taking reorders from stores around the city, sometimes returning several times in a week to some of the smaller shops to pick up late checks. With no car, we traveled by foot, subway, bus, and the occasional taxi. All our customers were within a few miles of the shop. I loved the idea of living in such a small village compared to the giant sprawl of Los Angeles where I was dead without a car.

I was also completely wrong about what would and wouldn't sell. The common variety black-and-white celebrity and psychedelic posters were the bread and butter of the wholesale and retail businesses. Our customers wanted Che Guevara, W.C. Fields, Bob Dylan, and black-light posters they could trip on. Everyone admired the art posters and the Czech movie posters. But no one bought the exotic posters. Few bought the Beardsley drawings or Toulouse-Lautrec posters. Even the solarized portraits of John, Paul, George, and Ringo languished unsold. Some said the Beatles were in a slump again, they had peaked. We continued to play the *Magical Mystery Tour* album over and over because Oskar had only been able to afford one album when he bought the record player, and he never got around to buying more.

In spite of the increased traffic in the store, Oskar fell farther behind in his bills, and yet, he remained upbeat, always smiling, always joking, always on the prowl for new people to support his business endeavors in one way or another.

I ran myself ragged keeping up. The whirl of the business and Oskar's energy kept me from thinking too much about my own fate, the war, and the sobering reality that I had yet to write anything worthwhile since crossing the border.

I quickly learned the hustle of business wasn't for me, but I continued to show up every day, mainly because by then Oskar had worked his way into the inner circle of hard-partying Québécois filmmakers and artists through a close friendship with a beautiful, high-energy, redhead named Suzelle Carle. Suzelle, in her thirties, was married to Gilles Carle, one of a handful of new Québécois film directors who were beginning to create a distinctly Québécois cinema. [5] [6]

Suzelle was an equally powerful force and trendsetter in the arts community. She owned Boutique Soleil in Old Montreal. Her shop sold a strange mix of leading edge art and sculpture and a line of high fashion knitwear which Suzelle's sister designed and manufactured. [7]

The first of Gilles Carle's independent feature films, *Le viol d'une jeune fille douce* (*The Rape of a Sweet Young Girl*), was still being edited that spring.

It was a quirky, black comedy about gangsters and outsiders. Carle and most of the other Québécois filmmakers were auteurs: writing, directing, and often acting in their own films. They didn't need writers, especially one who could work only in English, but it was thrilling to run with this crowd. There was always a party, fashion show, film screening, *vernissage*, restaurant, or bar to go to. I tagged along with Oskar and Suzelle often into the middle of the night, sleeping a few hours, and bouncing up in the morning to open the shop and begin the workday.

Poor Andrew kept saying he was getting better, but to me he appeared to be getting frailer by the week. He always had trouble breathing. He definitely couldn't keep up with Oskar and Suzelle. He made friends with a couple I introduced him to, a young poet, Arty Gold, and his much older roommate, Mary. Thankfully, Andrew continued to pay both halves of the rent on the apartment he shared with Oskar.

I wrote to my mother that I was most thankful not to be in the States any longer. "The stories we hear up here are horrifying, and everyone who comes back [from the US] says the summer [there] will be all war and no love. Well, Washington killed the love and peace generation so let's see what they are going to do with the angry young man. The politicians have asked for it this time, and they are really going to get it whether they like it or not."

I casually added, "By the way, I received my delinquency notice from the draft board. I should be inducted in about another month or so. *C'est la vie.*"

I began to contact a few more of my old friends in the States. I wanted desperately to hang onto my ties to the old country even though I believed I had cut myself off forever. I couldn't shake off being American as fast as I once thought.

CHAPTER 10

I RECEIVED MY preliminary work permit during the second week of March, four months after I had arrived in Montreal. My application was still "under investigation" by the Canadian government in Ottawa, but I could work.

I felt an enormous sense of relief. I let myself believe for the first time that I wouldn't be kicked out. All I had left to prove was that I could support myself.

I immediately got a couple of small freelance jobs from a friend of Emile's, Jean-Claude Pilon, writing English applications for film projects for the Canadian government in Ottawa. A tall, clean-shaven, quiet, and thoughtful intellect in his early thirties with light brown hair and an easygoing manner, Jean-Claude owned a small film company, Cinéclair, on St. Catherine Street near Guy. He was a veteran of the National Film Board like Gilles Carle. He made corporate and government films on contract and edited films from other producers. In the back room, he had many hours of film he had shot and planned to make into a feature documentary on the wild horses on Sable Island, a small, uninhabited island off the coast of Nova Scotia. All he needed was time and money.

Jean-Claude didn't have much work for me, but it helped supplement the meager income from the poster business. Once my work permit came through, I started drawing the same forty dollars a week that Oskar was drawing whenever the business could spare it.

"We can make a lot of money at this, and then you can go back to writing," Oskar assured me. I wanted to believe him. I kept reminding myself that I had spent the best part of the past four months with nothing to do but write and I had turned out nothing of worth. I had no great story to tell. I wondered if I ever would. Sometimes I thought the only thing driving me to want to be a writer was the constant dialogue in my head that never shut off.

"It's all about making money," Oskar insisted. "Then, everything else falls into place."

Oskar was a master of charm, a whirlwind of energy and bright ideas, always on the verge of something big, not just in posters, in anything. He talked two hairdressers, who owned a salon and a disco, into selling him their two-year-old Citroën DS executive model on credit with nothing down, so we could drive around town in style. Oskar sold us to the hairdressers as interior designers and said we would help redesign their club and a new hair salon.

"You have to make everyone feel good," Oskar told me. He was always smiling.

✶ ✶ ✶

On March 31, 1968, while I was working late with Oskar at the poster shop, I heard the news over the radio of President Johnson telling the world: "I shall not seek, nor will I accept the nomination of my party for another term as your President."

I had been following the US elections closely. Still, Johnson's decision was a surprise in a month of surprises. Senator Eugene McCarthy ran a close second to Johnson in the Democratic primary in New Hampshire on March 12 as an anti-war candidate. McCarthy's strong showing had also prompted New York Senator Robert Kennedy, a much better known figure than McCarthy, to enter the race on March 16. Two months previously, Bobby Kennedy had declared he would not run. Now he, too, was in the race.

✶ ✶ ✶

I was equally excited and intrigued by the changes taking place at the top in Canada. The federal government's young, hip Justice Minister, Pierre Elliott Trudeau, was running for leader of the Liberal Party to succeed the fatherly Prime Minister Lester Pearson, who was retiring. The Liberal Party Convention was on April 6. Trudeau was the dark horse candidate.

Trudeau was ultracool. The 48-year-old bachelor Cabinet Minister drove a 300SL Mercedes convertible and had the same kind of glamor and youth appeal as President Kennedy.

As Justice Minister, Trudeau had overseen legislation that had legalized contraception, abortion, and lotteries; decriminalized homosexual acts between consenting adults; provided new restrictions on gun ownership; and liberalized divorce laws. My friends thought it likely that Trudeau might extend personal choice to smoking marijuana. More important to me, Trudeau seemed unlikely to change the Liberal government's policy of allowing American draft resisters to stay in Canada and become legal immigrants. The Conservatives, on the other hand, didn't appear as favorably disposed to draft resisters.

Trudeau was also close friends with both Gilles and Suzelle Carle. With Trudeau a possibility in Canada, and Kennedy and McCarthy in the race in the US, I felt a rising sense of hope.

Then, more gunshots in America.

CHAPTER 11

THE ASSASSINATION OF Dr. Martin Luther King, Jr. in Memphis on April 4, 1968 took my breath away. I was at the shop when the news came over the radio.

America is insane. We're at war with ourselves, I told myself with a heavy heart.

King's death made me feel even more strongly that I had made the right decision to go to Canada. It also drove home the point that I still felt and thought like an American. I wondered if I always would.

✳ ✳ ✳

Two days after King was shot in the US, Trudeau won the leadership of the Liberal Party and became Prime Minister of Canada.

✳ ✳ ✳

Three days after King's assassination, I received a very warm letter from Jennifer in California telling me about the many things that had changed in her life.

I had known Jennifer for less than a month, but it came at a very intense and crucial time in my life—right before I left the US for Canada. Jennifer was a serious social activist who wanted to help the downtrodden. She had the same classes as me in the UCLA School of Social Work grad program. I was drawn to her immediately, not only because she was attractive but because she was intelligent and curious, and at the same time, gentle and warm, someone with whom I felt instantly close. She had a boyfriend, but she was interested in me, I think, mainly because I told her right off that I was writer and painter and was only in graduate school to keep out of the draft.

We both hated the war. Neither of us knew what to do about it.

Jennifer was also the first, seemingly sane, middle-class person I knew who talked about the country going so far downhill that kids like us would need to arm ourselves and go to war against the government.

She had gone out for a few years with a black guy while she was at the University of Chicago. She knew of blacks stockpiling guns for self-defense.

I lied the last time I saw her. I said I was dropping out of UCLA and returning to New Jersey for family reasons. I never told her I was heading to Canada.

After six months of silence, a student from UCLA passed through the shop one day. On a whim, I gave him her telephone number and said to call her and give her my address at the poster store. "Tell her I'm okay."

She had gone through as much change in her life as I had. Jennifer wrote that she had broken up with her old boyfriend and dropped out of grad school. She was now living in San Pedro, the seedy harbor area of Los Angeles.

She was organizing local members of the Students for a Democratic Society (SDS) in her neighborhood and working in a garment factory. "School had become unbearable," she said. She had gotten fed up with the "liberal bourgeois" trying to channel her into the system. She had changed her ideas about political activities enormously and had begun to realize what revolution in the country had to mean and what kinds of things had to be done. "Best not to write more," she ended that paragraph.

I remembered the morning she heard that Che Guevara had been executed in a jungle in Bolivia while we were in our first days of UCLA grad school together.

When I met Jennifer, I didn't know who Che Guevara was. Six months later, I was selling several dozen posters a week with Guevara's face emblazoned on them.

"How is your French?" she asked. "What kind of world are you living in? I hope it is political."

She wrote that she still had a couple of paintings I'd made the previous summer. They were hanging in her new apartment. "Everyone is constantly asking about them." She ended by asking me, "Will I ever see you again??? Write. Love, Jennifer."

Her words felt warm, loving, and uplifting. I tried to picture how enraged, how powerless and frustrated she must have felt when she heard of Martin Luther King's assassination. She had written her letter before the assassination.

I wrote back, telling her, "Get the hell out of the States, come to Canada, and start over in a fresh country."

I wondered what would happen if everyone my age and against the war just packed up and left for Canada.

★ ★ ★

I met Margaux at a dinner party at Daniel's new art studio, which he'd created out of an old movie theater. Margaux was an easy-going, dark-haired Francophone with long legs, narrow eyes, and dimples when she smiled, which was most of the time. I liked her right away. She was pleasant. She made everyone laugh and was a good listener. She worked in the film industry on the production side.

She offered to drive me home after the dinner party. I invited her in. She said yes without hesitating and stayed most of the night.

She left me exhausted and feeling liberated at four in the morning. "I have to leave early to get to the set," she said. She was working on a beer commercial. When she returned to my place at seven that evening, she wanted to go straight to bed and make love.

"I like you a lot, but I'm not in love with you," I warned her, a little worried that I had given her the wrong impression.

"I know. We're just having fun."

She was a couple of years older than me. She wanted to be in love but not with me.

"I was deeply in love with a wonderful man recently," she told me over dinner. "He's ten years older than me. Married. Still in love with his wife. For a moment, I let myself dream that he was in love with me. I think he loved me a little. Then, it was over. I'm not going to be in love again like that for a long time."

"How do you know?"

"I just know."

When we stopped seeing each other after a week, I felt both a loss and a sense of relief. I loved love as much as I loved sex. But I still wanted both.

Some sexual revolution, I thought. So easy to fall in love, but finding the right person and staying in love remained as elusive as ever—at least for me.

I inked my first international business deal at the beginning of April shortly after Peter Lebensold wandered into our gallery. The tall, handsome, blond-haired founder, editor, and publisher of the very hip film magazine *Take One* came to see Oskar to talk about distribution for his magazine in the UK. [8]

By the spring of 1968, Peter had pretty good distribution across Canada and the US. But his magazine was still too small to get a good distributor internationally. He was looking for an alternate solution.

I thought of Garry's girlfriend in London. Garry and his girlfriend were two of my old friends from Los Angeles. Garry had moved to London at the end of the summer of '67. He was working for the UK branch of his uncle's film company, American International Pictures (AIP), reading scripts and writing some sort of schlocky sex film for them—his description—and sending articles on the virtues of marijuana to the British underground periodical *Oz*. His girlfriend had followed him to England and was waiting for her work permit so she could teach drama in a London school similar to Summerhill.

Peter and Oskar were willing to give any idea a try, and I soon had Garry's girlfriend riding around London on her bike taking orders for *Take One* from hip London bookstores, magazine outlets, and art-house movie theaters.

"You have a knack for business," Oskar told me.

I wasn't so sure. I didn't share the same hunger for risk that Oskar did. He was like a shark moving through the city, running the business during the day, and out the rest of the time looking for people who had money or connections.

He loved selling.

I wanted to get back to creating my own world. I needed to write. I began wrestling with staying home and working on a low-budget film script that I had been developing or hanging around with Oskar, Suzelle,

Gilles, and their friends hoping that the experiences I was having would lead to something worth writing about one day.

I also continued to try to understand what it meant to be Canadian. I wondered what it would mean to me if Quebec separated from the rest of Canada. The only Canada I knew was Montreal.

I would probably move on. I was the foreigner, an outsider.

One thing I noticed that was different, Canadians didn't identify themselves in terms of war and their history. They had no George Washington, no Abraham Lincoln, no Teddy Roosevelt. They had no Revolution, no Davy Crockett, no Alamo, no Gettysburg. They didn't worship their own history. They didn't even have their own flag until 1965. Hardly anyone knew the national anthem. An ideal place, I thought, to become a citizen of the world if only I could shed my American skin.

Whatever else Gilles Carle felt about Quebec sovereignty, he could not have been more excited about Trudeau, who had dined often at their house.

When my brother and sister-in-law came to Montreal for the Easter weekend, the Carles invited all of us to Easter dinner. Gilles related with a childlike glee how surreal it felt to be able to call the Prime Minister on the phone and say, "Pierre. *Comment* ça va?"

"Looks like you're doing all right for yourself," my brother told me, impressed that I was hanging out with friends of Trudeau.

My brother brought my Gibson acoustic guitar from New Jersey. I didn't realize how much I had missed it until I tuned it for the first time in months and began to play.

I began turning a few of my poems into songs. [9]

On April 20, Pierre Elliott Trudeau was officially sworn in as Canada's fifteenth Prime Minister.

Two days later, I went to the immigration office and became an official landed immigrant of Canada.

CHAPTER 12

ON APRIL 23, 1968, my first full day as an official landed immigrant in Canada, Prime Minister Trudeau called a general election, promising a "Just Society" and featuring campaign slogans like, "Come work with me" and "Vote for New Leadership for All of Canada."

Trudeau was a committed federalist. He believed in a strong central government and a united Canada.

The Conservatives, led by Federal Opposition Leader, Robert Stanfield, the former seventeenth Premier of Nova Scotia, started out with a policy of *deux nations*—the idea that Canada was made up of two nations, one French and one English. [10]

My mother wrote wondering what would happen to me if Canada started a draft. I didn't know.

The initial popularity of the Conservatives began to shrink under the weight of "Trudeaumania," a play on "Beatlemania," which it resembled. Canada became more infatuated with Trudeau the more they saw of him. It felt to me like it had when I was fifteen and the handsome, youthful Senator John F. Kennedy ran for President. Trudeau's public appearances took on the aura of a rock concert and Love-In, complete with screaming young women—something never seen before in Canadian politics. Trudeau's glamor spilled onto the front pages of American and European newspapers and magazines.

Trudeau, only two years younger than President Kennedy would have been if still alive, was my new Kennedy. I wanted him to win. I wanted to be in a country where the top guy made sense when he spoke.

☆ ☆ ☆

Suzelle's affair with Oskar began to unravel at the end of April. I had no
trouble understanding why. Oskar was jumping into bed with every
pretty woman who threw herself at him. He was also borrowing heavily
from Suzelle and some of her friends. I remained close to both of them
but found myself drifting toward Suzelle. I trusted her more.

Suzelle confided in me one night over dinner at Chez Delmo's that
Gilles had been having an affair while making *Le viol d'une jeune fille douce.*
Apparently, everyone knew about his affair but me, which was under-
standable because much of the conversation that swirled around me
when I was with the Carles and their friends was in French. I still didn't
understand French very well.

"Do you love Oskar?" I asked.

"No. I enjoy him. He reminds me a little of Gilles in his twenties." Oskar was payback to Gilles for his affair.

Weeks later, I learned that Gilles had been having his affair with Margaux.

CHAPTER 13

WITH MONEY COMING in occasionally from the shop and a little from free-lancing, I started thinking about getting a bigger place. Suzelle told me about a couple of artists who were moving out of a three-bedroom flat on St. Urbain Street a couple of blocks north of Sherbrooke Street.

The flat was the top floor of a two-story old stone row house with its own outside door and inside staircase to the second floor. The living space was huge—two bedrooms on the street side, a spacious living room, a third bedroom off the living room, and a large kitchen at the back, two steps down from the living room. The ceilings were nine feet high. The doors had little windows over them to help circulate the air.

On the negative side, the hardwood floors were so slanted that I felt the building might be in danger of collapsing. Large patches of plaster had fallen out of the walls and ceiling in several spots. The bathroom and kitchen hadn't been touched for forty or fifty years and were on their last legs, much like the rundown places I'd lived in for the past four years in Los Angeles. I was confident I could coax a little more life out of the apartment.

The rent was seventy dollars a month, fifteen dollars more than I had been paying for my basement room. I also had to pay for oil heating, gas for the stove, electricity, and telephone. I told myself if I ran into trouble, I could rent out a room or two to help cover the costs. The landlords were an elderly Polish couple who had come to Canada after the war. They lived in one of the other adjoining row houses. The husband owned a small travel agency on the Main two blocks away that specialized in travel between Poland and Canada. He didn't care what I did with the place as long as I paid the rent.

The previous tenants sold me their old refrigerator and ancient gas stove for thirty-five dollars and tossed in for free their old jewelry making table—a long, narrow slab of inch-thick marble about two-and-a-half-feet wide by nine-feet long that sat on two large wooden tea chests. It was my only piece of furniture for my first few days in the empty, old apartment.

I lived off of sandwiches and juice, and slept on the floor for a couple of nights before buying a brass bed for twenty-five dollars and a dresser for another fifteen at a junk-filled secondhand store on the Main. The owner threw in an old mattress and box spring for nothing.

I needed to set up house to feel settled.

I'm staying here, I told myself.

★ ★ ★

Three weeks passed before I heard from Jennifer again.

Her job at a hellhole factory was a real shock to her. She talked of revolution in the US, led by the working class. She had been pressed so hard by her supervisor she had sewed her finger with a machine. Raising interest in a union had turned out to be more difficult than she imagined. "It's hard to recruit the women because most speak only Spanish or Japanese, and their political consciousness is almost non-existent."

I wondered what she would have thought of my father's old glove factory. I wondered what she would think of me if she knew I wasn't trying to organize anyone.

I struggled with what I should tell her.

Was I morally defective because I didn't want to fight in Vietnam or in Jennifer's war? Was I wrong in believing that soldiers were all expendable and it wouldn't matter which side I was on? Were the Red Chinese, who had gone into peaceful Tibet and decimated the population, to be admired? What about the bloody and vicious Cultural Revolution already underway in China where Mao's Red Guards were busy destroying the last of the educated liberals and turning the country upside down? What of the Russians who had brutally stamped out the Hungarian Revolt?

Were the Chinese and Russians really more admirable than the US in Vietnam? Was Cuba an utopia or just another hellhole run by a new type of dictator?

All soldiers were the first victims of war, I thought. The way to honor your dead soldiers is to make sure that your new soldiers never have to fight in a meaningless war.

How could I ever say anything meaningful about war—and this war in particular—without sounding glib and full of self-interest? Who would listen?

⋆ ⋆ ⋆

The perfect words finally came in the form of a sign. Literally.

The closest movie theater to my new flat was *Cinéma de l'Élysée*, a French-language repertory movie theater just a few blocks south of me on Milton Street just off the Main. It often showed double bills of old movies. The neighborhood had once been the heart of the old Montreal Jewish ghetto at the turn of the century. The building housing the cinema had once been one of the largest synagogues in the ghetto.

I had been there with Suzelle and Gilles to see a private screening of Gilles' film before it went to the Berlin Film Festival. I had also seen a half-dozen French-language films there by myself to try to improve my French.

One day while walking past the theater, I noticed a new film being advertised—*La guerre est finie*. [11] I knew enough French to realize in a second what it meant. *La guerre est finie* translated to "The War Is Over" or "War Is Over."

That's what I want, I thought each time I passed the marquee. I want the war to be over.

The film title summed up what I had done. I hadn't joined a political group before or after I made the leap into the unknown. I came to Canada as a singular act of defiance between me and the current government of the United States. I was a realist, an idealist, a pragmatist, an absurdist, an existentialist, a coward, or anything I had to be. My only message was, "Just walk away if you can; declare the war over. Don't go to hell if you don't have to."

CHAPTER 14

OSKAR AND I opened a second poster shop in Old Montreal after Oskar talked the landlord into letting him have the first month for free. Oskar also found a new steady girlfriend—a young, tall, elegant, recent immigrant from the Philippines who followed him like a puppy. He started spending more time with her and less on the business, leaving me to service the accounts and run the shops with an assistant.

I was clearly worried about the business. We were picking up new wholesale accounts, but we weren't paying our bills or ourselves.

Oskar insisted, "You worry too much. Business will get better as soon as the tourists show up."

We waited anxiously for the first tourist season after Expo. Some of the old World's Fair buildings had been reconfigured into permanent exhibitions. Battered retailers across the city were hoping for a boost in tourism after the deep winter slump. I couldn't stop worrying. I was nearly broke again. My rent was coming due.

When Suzelle told me about Robert Russel, a friend of hers who might have some writing work in English for me, I jumped at the chance.

Robert Russel owned Orbafilm. It was located on the third floor of a turn-of-the-century office building at 418 St. Sulpice Street. The building backed onto the Notre-Dame de Québec Basilica, a landmark cathedral in Place d'Armes Square, a seventeenth-century plaza where soldiers and militia assembled to defend the town.

During the day, the neighborhood smelled of chocolate from a small confectionery factory around the corner on St. Paul Street.

Gilles and Robert Russel had been at the National Film Board together. Russel was a tall, slim, distinguished-looking man just shy of forty with large, trendy glasses, longish, dark hair, and a friendly smile.

"Orbafilm isn't making movies or TV productions anymore," Russel explained as he showed me around his suite of rooms occupying the entire third floor of the building. His own office was a large room at the front with windows overlooking the street. The front room was arranged as a combination office and studio apartment with couches, cushioned armchairs, a coffee table, a desk, and several bookcases crammed with books and magazines.

"We're creating the next medium," Russel said. "We're just getting started."

The next medium, he continued, was "demand communications." Russel had already coined the term and written about the concept in *Take One*, the film magazine that Peter Lebensold published. [12]

Russel was building one of the first practical applications of the concepts of communications guru, Marshall McLuhan—an advanced information service and an early warning system on global change for world leaders and senior executives in business and government.

Russel's idea was simple. His writers read the most respected newspapers and periodicals in the world and selected the most important stories on new technologies, new ideas, trends, and forecasts. Selected articles were clipped and filed under one of sixteen subject headings.

Why only newspapers and periodicals? Simple. Books took two or more years to write and publish. By the time they came out, they were out-of-date. "All the new ideas, trends, technologies, and products show up in newspapers and periodicals faster than books," Russel explained.

Russel had been selling information packages to governments and large corporations for several years. He had so much business at one time that he had employed a half-dozen writers in the middle room of the office suite. Copyright issues had forced him to shut down that version of his service. He was currently developing a new type of service using abstracts to get around the copyright laws. He had one writer working with him, Arthur, a fellow about my age with glasses, pale skin, and dark hair. [13]

Russel was presently negotiating a large contract to supply information to one of the departments of the federal government in Ottawa. It was a large pilot project that he believed would be adapted by the new government, regardless of which party won the next election in a few weeks. He was so well connected he had direct access to both Trudeau and Stanfield through close friends and family. He was gearing up to have enough material on hand to launch his latest service.

Walking me into the cavernous unfinished back room, Russel showed me the rows of filing cabinets where he stored his clippings and publications. "Someday, all this will be stored on computers, and you'll be able to access everything from anywhere in the world."

Each abstract he or Arthur wrote from the constant stream of articles they selected was keyworded. All you would have to do in the future was punch in a word or two on your computer keyboard and everything on that subject would appear on a screen on your desk. Russel was working on experiments with a computer company on storing articles by keywords. At the moment, all the articles were accessed by hand through his filing system.

"Anyone who expects to effectively run a major corporation or government needs to be aware of change everywhere in the new global village," Russel explained.

Everything Russel told me sounded fascinating, particularly after he offered me a chance to work for him.

"You'll be getting in on the ground floor of a new business. We're creating the future."

I wanted to be part of this.

The pay was only forty-five dollars a week, only a few cents above Quebec's minimum wage per hour but five dollars more than I had been drawing from the poster business—or rather what I should have been drawing if Oskar had the money to pay me.

I was about three weeks behind in my draw when I told Oskar I was leaving to work for Orbafilm. For once, he didn't try to talk me into staying. I was a little surprised since he was always so upbeat about our future together.

"And don't worry about the money I owe you, Joseph. I'll have it in a day or two."

Two days later, Oskar and his girlfriend vanished without a trace.

CHAPTER 15

OSKAR LEFT BEHIND two stores, the Citroën DS, and a mound of debts. Some people were so mad at him that one or two of our acquaintances wondered whether Oskar might be fish bait at the bottom of the St. Lawrence River.

Thankfully, no one was mad at me or thought I was responsible for any of his debts. If anything, most people felt sorry for me, as they knew Oskar also owed me money.

I promised myself to be more cautious and less naïve in the future, and I also told myself not to worry. I would make it somehow. I had a new job in a crazy new company.

I bought a few more secondhand items for next to nothing to fill my rambling, empty house—an iron-frame bed and mattress for the little bedroom, a couple of wooden rocking chairs, a small desk, an old, painted pine washstand, an oak dresser, an old settee that could function as a couch or guest bed, and a pair of candelabras that came from a nearby decommissioned convent.

I felt settled enough to send away for a subscription to *The Evergreen Review* and begin a new relationship.

★ ★ ★

I met Laura, a slim, petite woman with long, silky, straight, dark hair, a radiant smile, and dark eyes, at a party. She was studying science at McGill.

She made beautiful, long, colorful curtains for the front windows of my L-shaped room and read my old novel. She thought it was strangely compelling and twisted. For a few days, I tried rewriting it again. It was no use. It was part of my past.

I worked harder on my film script and began another one. Being in love made it easier to stay out of the downtown bars and remain home and work.

I heard from more old friends from California. John, one of my close actor friends from Los Angeles, had been deferred again from the draft. We had talked often about leaving the US together and going to Canada before I finally took off on my own. John had won his latest deferment after a bad motorcycle accident while driving through the Hollywood Hills on a rainy winter night. He took a nasty spill on a slick patch of road and cut his knee to the bone. He had just made his first Hollywood film and was sure his knee injury would keep him out of the war until he was too old to be called up. It felt strange to be happy that he had been injured badly enough to avoid the war.

Sparky and Kaye were madly in love and wrestling with her parents who didn't think Sparky was ready to get married—because he hadn't finished his degree, had no money, and hadn't fulfilled his military obligations. Kaye's father had been in the US Air Force during World War II and currently worked for the military-industrial complex. Sparky was killing himself trying to make enough money to stay in school full time at UC Berkeley, a necessity to keep his student deferment. Sparky had applied for Conscientious Objector status as a hedge. He also had gone to a psychiatrist to create a paper trail to show he was too mentally unstable to go into the military. Even if neither plan worked, the appeals would still delay his induction by a couple of years.

Jeff, my old roommate and biology lab partner at USC, had a deferment because he was married and had a year-old son. He had an exemption but had applied to immigrate to Canada with his wife, Cindy, and their toddler. Like Garry, who had left the US for England, Jeff couldn't stand the war.

Jennifer's latest letter from California was tender but full of growing frustration at the world she was living in. She explained that it was a difficult period for her to write. The only thing of meaning, she insisted, is to be "a Marxist-Leninist."

She tried to explain that it was a whole way of life and a way to live, and she was in the process of unlearning "twenty-three years of bourgeois bullshit" in order to become a radical.

Every day at the factory, she insisted, she was becoming a little more aware.

Conditions, presumably for the unmentioned revolution, were growing, and she predicted a lot would be happening soon.

"So babe, keep writing and I'll try again soon. Love, Jennifer."

I sensed I might not hear from her again. I was okay with that. I had to find my own footing in my new home.

Laura and I spent a lot of time together.

She was warm, funny, beautiful, and intelligent. Like all the Montreal girls I had met, regardless of ethnic background or religion, sex was something the women felt comfortable with, like wine at dinner. They dressed and moved to highlight their sensuality. Sex was easy, fun. It made it easy for us to be in love.

Her parents didn't share her enthusiasm for me. They thought I was the devil incarnate, a dirty hippie-freak, corrupting their daughter.

Actually, Laura and I were corrupting each other. We were eager to believe that love was our birthright, that it would solve everything.

It solved nothing, of course.

Once again, the guns of America ripped through my fragile psyche and made my skin crawl.

Senator Robert Kennedy. Shot. Dead.

The assassination of his brother, President John F. Kennedy, four years before had left me broken and in shock. I thought I had healed and hardened. I hadn't. I now felt the same shock, the same disorientation, the same sense of foreboding.

The shooting of Robert Kennedy on June 5, 1968 and his death on June 6 seemed to break things inside me, not least of which was the ingrained belief that America was a shining beacon of light that had simply lost its way.

I suddenly knew better. It was a land capable of eating its own children.

I instructed my brother to sell my antique gun and sword collection and send me the money.

CHAPTER 16

IN THE MIDDLE of June, a scare story began circulating through the underground throughout California. The stars had aligned just right for a giant cataclysm of some kind. Some thought the pending disaster was linked to a recent 100-megaton H-bomb test explosion in Utah two months before as well as to recent rumors of UFO sightings. All signs pointed to giant earthquakes and volcanos erupting on the coming Saturday. The seers were predicting California would fall into the ocean. Sparky and Kaye sent me a special delivery letter to get out of Montreal. They were worried our extinct volcano in the center of the island might erupt. They were heading to the eastern slope of the Rockies in Colorado.

Laura and I spent the weekend at my place barely a stone's throw from the epicenter of the volcano's core. On Sunday afternoon, we lay in bed listening to the military band housed in the office building across the street rehearsing show tunes like "Mame" and "Hello, Dolly." We laughed about how Sparky and Kaye must be feeling, sitting on the eastern slope of the Rockies with a bag of grass, smoking themselves into silliness, realizing the world was not ready to end.

✳ ✳ ✳

This war is different, I told myself. The GIs in Vietnam are listening to the same music everyone is listening to in North America and Europe. It's calling the soldiers home. Was it possible that enough people my own age could put a stop to war by demanding that it stop?

✳ ✳ ✳

The 1968 Presidential race for the White House swung into full gear over the summer. It made everyone nervous. As both parties geared up for the fight, my mother wrote, "If you see a way out, write and tell the world."

She added, "It's good that you have three bedrooms. Maybe we'll all have to come up there!"

✳ ✳ ✳

I met Zeke and Candice one night while playing guitar and singing on amateur night at a coffeehouse on the corner of Notre-Dame and Bonsecours.

They called me over to their table after I'd finished my set, introduced themselves, and offered to buy me a coffee.

"We liked your songs," Zeke told me.

"I can't keep a beat, my voice is weak, and I can easily lose the tune," I freely admitted.

"Yes, but you have a way with words," Candice insisted.

Zeke and Candice lived a block down the street in an apartment overlooking the Sailors' Church.

Candice was my age with soft, dark hair, rosy cheeks, and big luminous eyes. She and Zeke had been drawn to Montreal by Expo the previous year. She was from Seattle and an actress. She was in the running for a TV series for the Canadian Broadcasting Corporation (CBC), Canada's public TV network. She also modeled with one of the top agencies.

Zeke worked in publishing. He was four years older than me and from Toronto. He was tall, fair-skinned, wore glasses, and had receding reddish-brown hair. He had a friendly manner and an easy laugh. He had briefly played Canadian football for the Toronto Argonauts.

Both Zeke and Candice were eager to work in the movie business.

I told them I'd been working on a script.

"I'm always interested in reading something new, Joseph. Right now, I'm getting ready to shoot a small film of my own."

I was all ears. "What's it about?"

"I haven't quite finished the script. All I can tell you is Candice is lining up some of her friends to be in it."

"Tell me about your publishing job," I asked, always on the lookout for possible new opportunities.

"It's just a corporate job, a way to bring in some money while I'm working my way into public affairs."

"Zeke would make a great TV reporter, don't you think?" Candice asked.

"Yes," I said. But his current day job had caught my interest. I persisted. "So what kind of publishing company are you working for? I'm always looking to pick up extra gigs. I worked on a textbook at university. I'm working in a think tank writing abstracts of articles on the future right now. No writing job is beneath me."

"I don't think you'd want to write for us, Joseph."

"Why not? What's the name of your company?"

Zeke just smiled.

"Go on. Tell him," Candice said.

"The Globe Newspaper Group. You've never heard of it." He kept exchanging glances with Candice. I wanted to be let in on their private joke, especially since The Globe Newspaper Group sounded so impressive.

"What do they publish?"

Zeke leaned closer and lowered his voice. "Tabloids." He laughed. Candice laughed.

I remained intensely curious. "What kind of tabloids?"

"Have you ever heard of *Midnight*?"

It took me a second to realize I recognized the name. I had seen copies of it. It was a lurid, weekly tabloid newspaper that appeared prominently displayed at newsstands and in the little mom-and-pop grocery stores across the city alongside of the *National Enquirer*. Both sported freaky and outrageous headlines about celebrities doing crazy things and weird human interest stories, including UFO sightings that were obviously fabricated. I had seen a French version called *Minuit* with the same logo, headlines, and cover photos as *Midnight*.

"You work for *Midnight*?" I asked.

Zeke raised his eyebrows apologetically. "It pays the rent, Joseph. I've been trying to break into the CBC for more than a year. You have no idea how many stories I've already submitted. They've all been turned down. I'm doing what I can to keep my head above water."

He thought I was looking down on what he was doing.

"I meant—wow—you work for *Midnight?*" Anyone working in the English publishing business in Montreal was intriguing to me. "What do you do there?"

"I'm an articles editor."

"What's that?"

"I hunt for stories from newspapers around the world."

It sounded like a crazy version of what Bob Russel was doing. My mind whirled. I smelled opportunity. "How does it work?"

"When we spot a good story or photo in another newspaper, we hire the original writer under the table to rewrite it in a new version exclusively for us, or we buy the photos and make up our own story to go with it."

"Like stories about UFOs?"

He laughed.

"What about the celebrity stories? Most of those are fake, right?"

"Fake, or shall we say, embellished."

"Don't you get sued?"

"Not very often."

He gave me several reasons. "Most people simply don't believe what they read in the tabloids. Most celebrities in Hollywood believe that any publicity is good publicity. They take the tabloids for granted as a necessary good and evil."

A lot of what *Midnight* and the other tabloids wrote was protected by the First Amendment in the US, where, Zeke explained, they sold ninety percent of their newspapers. *Midnight* was the second-largest weekly tabloid in the US after the *National Enquirer*. "We create entertainment. Think of the tabloids like the media's version of professional wrestling. We're held to lower standards and allowed to exist as long as we don't cause a war or a run on a bank."

Zeke had been working for The Globe Newspaper Group for several months. The regal-sounding publishing company put out *Midnight* and several other equally lurid tabloids, which had been purchased with profits from *Midnight's* success in the past decade and a half. The English-language tabloids were written, edited, and published in Canada and sold across North America. The French-language version sold throughout Quebec and other cities and towns in other Canadian provinces with large Francophone populations.

I was fascinated.

"We use a lot of freelancers. If you're interested, I could see if one of the editors needs another writer."

"I'm definitely interested."

I told myself the stories were a form of lowbrow adult satire, not much different really than a working man's *Mad* magazine or Paul Krassner writing his crazy stories in *The Realist*. I was game for anything. I wondered what it would be like to write shocking tabloid stories.

Any extra income would also help. Orbafilm had a large, pending contract about to be signed in Ottawa, but until then, I was just squeaking by.

Zeke asked me for some samples of my writing to show to the editors. I gave him a short, first-person account of my experiences in the Watts Riots. My hometown Gannett newspaper in New Jersey had published it, calling it impressionistic. I also gave him a short story I had submitted to *The Evergreen Review* the previous year. The short story—a sketch of a man on a bad trip in Greenwich Village—had been called "authentic" by Seymour Krim, a contributing editor at the time to the *Review* who had championed my submission. It had also been called "disgusting and pointless" by managing editor Fred Jordan, who had rejected it. With those reviews, I imagined I might fit right into the tabloids.

"Someone will get back to you if they have an assignment."

✷ ✷ ✷

When I didn't hear from the Globe, I figured I just hadn't proved sordid enough and laughed it off, telling myself that I was too good for that kind of work anyway.

Soon, I hoped, Zeke would get his short film produced and that would set in motion a sequence of events leading to financing the feature film script I was currently working on.

✷ ✷ ✷

Zeke's dream of shooting a small film got closer to reality when he found a financial backer. The potential moneyman was a young, staid, recent Swiss-German immigrant, Matt Kunheim. Matt was making his fortune in the stock market and had a passion for films. His mother, Brigitte Helm, was one of the most famous actresses in pre-war German and international cinema. She was the star of Fritz Lang's 1927 masterpiece *Me-tropolis.* [14] Zeke and I harbored hopes that Matt might actually bankroll Zeke's short film and finance my film, too, or, at least, help raise the money once I finished the script. I was also hoping that some of Matt's stock market acumen would drift my way. I couldn't help wondering what Laura's mother would think of me if I became a success.

Success and Laura's mother suddenly took on new meaning. Only days before Laura's departure to Israel and Europe, she told me she had missed her period. "I think I might be pregnant."

CHAPTER 17

MY MOTHER WROTE to tell me my father's latest cryosurgery operation for his Parkinson's appeared to be successful. The pain and trembling on his left side were considerably reduced. His speech was slurred, but everyone seemed to believe that would improve over time with therapy.

On June 19, eight days after my father's operation, my brother and sister-in-law had a baby boy. I was an uncle for the first time.

Laura called me from the airport just before her plane took off on the start of her month-long tour. She was still "late." She had no address where I could write her while she was traveling. I had to rely on her letters until she returned.

"I love you and can't wait to see you," she said.

"I love you, too," I told her, wondering how my life would change if we got married and had a kid. I was both fascinated and scared to death of such a momentous possibility. The fear got the best of me most days. I was barely making enough to feed myself. I couldn't imagine being responsible for three people.

★ ★ ★

On the day before the national election Prime Minister Trudeau came to Montreal to sit in the grandstand and watch the annual Saint-Jean-Baptiste Day parade on Sherbrooke Street East.

The Feast Day of Saint-Jean-Baptiste had come to Quebec with the first French Colonists in the 1500s and had become a magnet for Quebec nationalists.

The young, radical Québécois hated Trudeau because he symbolized a united Canada.

During the festivities that evening, separatists began hurling rocks and bottles at the open reviewing stand where Trudeau was sitting. A crowd of separatist sympathizers chanted *"Trudeau au poteau"* (Trudeau to the gallows). Trudeau's security detail encircled the dignitaries and urged them to move to a safer location. Trudeau refused to go. He sat in his seat and ignored the missiles hurled by the mob.

Trudeau's stoic defiance was broadcast in newscasts across the country, influencing the election the next day. Trudeau's party, the Liberals, won the election, picking up an additional twenty-six parliamentary seats for a total of 154 out of 264, an 18.3 percent increase. It was enough to give Trudeau a solid majority government.

✷ ✷ ✷

My job at Orbafilm made me think about the world in ways I hadn't before. At university, I had done tons of research, digging through periodicals in psychology, sociology, and other fields, but I had never been much of a general newspaper or magazine reader. Suddenly, I was monitoring dozens of newspapers and magazines a day, looking for anything that might be used to predict the future.

We—Arthur and I, and sometimes Bob—read through *The New York Times, The Wall Street Journal, Financial Times* (London), *The Japan Times,* English translations of USSR publications and a German publication, a Red Chinese English-language magazine, *The Economist, Forbes, Fortune, Businessweek, Time, Newsweek, Scientific American, Architectural Digest, Journal of the American Medical Association, Evergreen Review, Playboy,* and the newly launched *Rolling Stone* magazine. Russel read *Le Monde* and *Corriere della Sera.*

We were futurists, Russel said. We were internationalists.

Montreal was well placed, Russel insisted, to be a center for pioneering work on the future. It was a part of the powerful, rich North American engine of science, technology, and innovation. It was bilingual. It was America's best friend and friendly to English and French. Corporate headquarters for many of Canada's most important businesses, including several banks and the telephone company, were located in Montreal. McGill University was world class in several fields. Expo '67 had high-

lighted new ways to improve human habitats by showcasing Buckminster Fuller's Geodesic Dome and Moshe Safdie's Habitat '67. Russel was
convinced that the forward-looking Québécois, like the new technocrats
who had gone with Trudeau to Ottawa to run Canada, would triumph
over the isolationists.

My work at Orbafilm was an acting job. I pretended I was a world
leader, a busy politician, a senior government bureaucrat, a titan of industry, and a new breed of global thinker. I needed to keep on top of important changes in technology and culture as each segment of society, the
economy, and other forces became more intertwined. I learned from Arthur that McLuhan had stayed at Russel's house when he visited Montreal. McLuhan had named Russel's company. [15] Russel had played an
important role in bringing together some very important global thinkers—all friends of his—for a conference centered around the twenty-fifth
anniversary of the National Film Board, including McLuhan; John Grier-
son, British filmmaker, founder of the NFB, and father of documentary
films; and Pierre Schaeffer, renowned communications innovator and
composer from Paris.

I was excited. I was part of the future.

CHAPTER 18

I WAS WRONG. I hadn't been rejected by *Midnight.* I got a phone call at Orbafilm one afternoon from John Vader, *Midnight's* editor, asking me to stop by.

The offices of The Globe Newspaper Group were on the sixth floor of a modern office building at 1440 St. Catherine Street West and Mackay Street near Guy.

The reception area was spacious and well appointed. It reminded me of the lobbies of the big advertising companies I had visited in New York with my Uncle Sam. This was no fly-by-night operation.

The receptionist was smartly dressed and wearing makeup. She led me down a long hallway, past other offices. At the end, we turned into a large, open room filled with men and women at desks, reading newspapers, talking on the phone, and typing away on upright typewriters.

Along one wall were doors to several smaller offices.

The windows along the far wall offered a panoramic view of the St. Lawrence River and the mountains of the Eastern Townships.

Zeke was on the phone at a desk in the middle of the bullpen, jotting notes on a yellow pad. He was too deep in conversation to notice me as I went by.

John Vader occupied a large corner office filled with bookcases and filing cabinets. His desk was buried under a sea of page proofs, typed stories ready to be edited, newspapers, and old copies of *Midnight,* which I had been reading on and off since I'd met Zeke.

John was in his mid-thirties, pale complexioned with a hint of a five o'clock shadow on his square jaw. Coke-bottle-thick glasses in heavy black frames sat partway down the bridge of his nose. The glasses magnified his heavy lidded eyes. He had a cigarette in one hand and a pencil in the other, both of which he put down as he stood to shake my hand across the desk.

He was an inch shorter than me and heavyset, maybe thirty or forty pounds heavier than me. It was hard to tell under the rumpled white shirt.

"Sit down. Don't be nervous. I'm not going to bite," he told me in a soft, deep voice as he waved me into the seat on the other side of his desk.

My overall impression was of a somewhat sleepy bear.

"So, you're Zeke's friend," he said.

"Yes."

"And he explained how we work?"

I nodded.

"You think you can write for *Midnight*?"

"I think so," I said, hoping I could. I was nervous and completely unsure of myself.

"Then, let's give it a try." His smile was comforting, encouraging. He handed me a photo from a folder on his desk.

It was a very gruesome black-and-white shot of a man lying across a railroad track after he had been run over by a train.

"The photo is from Mexico, from a stringer we know down there. He sends us photos no one else will publish."

The caption on a narrow slip of paper taped to the bottom of the photo was in Spanish. I studied it, trying to decipher what it said.

"Don't worry about the caption. We have our own story. The title is: 'Wife Caught Cheating. Husband Ties Wife's Lover to Railroad Tracks.' You fill in the rest. Just make it sound like the other stories we publish."

The photo and article would make up a half-page story for the next issue of the newspaper. Half-page articles paid five dollars apiece, full-page articles paid ten, and cover stories paid between fifteen and as much as twenty-five dollars if they covered a double-page spread inside.

I was full of trepidation, wondering whether or not I could write a credible fake story.

My half-page article required me to write about three-and-a-half double-spaced pages (about 800 to a 1,000 words) of bogus narrative and dialogue with made-up names, explaining how this imaginary husband had arrived home from work, found his wife in bed with her lover, flew into a rage, and tied the lover to the railroad track where said lover was cut in half by the train.

I went into a tailspin over the next few days.

I have gone to literary hell, I told myself. How could I possibly prostitute myself to write such a story? I wondered if I really didn't deserve to be in Vietnam getting shot at by Viet Cong.

I felt humiliated.

I also felt strangely frightened—after all my boasting, could I actually produce a story they would accept?

I read and reread all the copies of *Midnight* that John Vader had given me. I repeated the mantra that nobody could possibly take the articles in this newspaper seriously. It was, as Zeke said, journalism's answer to professional wrestling. It was nothing more than a lowbrow version of *The Realist* or any of a dozen other underground papers.

I felt overwhelmed, short of breath. Could I write fiction and be paid for it?

Just do it, I told myself. The money will come in handy, especially if the promised raise at Orbafilm doesn't come through, or, if Laura returns from Europe with a baby on the way.

The possibility that I would have to join the adult world and support a wife and child lit an immense fire under me, pushing me through all the self-doubts.

I gave it my best shot. I tried to make it sound as much like the other stories as I could. I dropped off the photo and my story at the reception desk of the Globe the next day, unsure how well I'd done, and unsure when John Vader would get around to reading it.

John Vader was the consummate gentleman. He would never keep a writer or photographer waiting any longer than he had to. He called me at Orbafilm at the end of the next day.

"Great job," he told me. "I can give you some more stories next week if you'd like."

"Definitely," I told him, feeling elated. I had passed. I had earned five dollars for my first bona fide published work of fiction. Eat your heart out, *Evergreen Review.*

"John thinks you're a really good writer," Zeke told me a few days later.

Apparently, I had whatever talent one needed to write crazy stories. The sheer irreverence of the work spurred me on. More freelance stories followed. The story lines were as crazy as the novel I had written the previous year, filled with impossible characters, escapes, near misses, and disasters. With a straight face, I wrote about a man who had been locked in the toilet for thirty years. Without a second thought, I wrote a mother's description of her adult son as his face caught fire from aftershave lotion. In my words, the victim's mother explained, "I looked up and John was lighting a cigarette. The next thing I knew his face exploded in flames. His hair and shirt caught fire and then he lost control of the car." The car, I added, careened off the road, crashed through a fence, and stopped after killing a cow.

I cashed my first checks.

I was a bona fide pulp fiction whore.

I hoped my readers would laugh and not take seriously anything I wrote.

I was also actively looking for something else to pay the bills. Bob Russel had delayed the raises for Arthur and me once more because the finishing touches were still being put on the contract in Ottawa. In spite of continuing delays, we were assured we would soon be up and running at full speed and expanding the business.

✷ ✷ ✷

Dr. Floyd Ruch tracked me down through my parents in New Jersey. During my senior year at USC, Ruch, my professor in industrial psychology, had hired me to write the workbook for the latest edition of *Psychology and Life,* the standard Psychology 101 textbook in most introductory college and university psychology courses in the US. The textbook had already gone through a half-dozen revisions and had been around for decades. Ruch was eager for me to write back because the latest edition of *Psychology and Life* was about to go to press. The publisher, Scott Foresman, needed a release from me. Ruch and I corresponded and talked on the phone. Ruch didn't seem the least bothered that I had taken off for Canada. "I'll keep you in mind if any new projects come up," he told me.

My mother wrote to tell me our family friend Billy was waiting out his trial in the brig, guarding other soldiers charged with being AWOL, desertion, and other offenses. Word on the street at the time was that on any given day in the US, twenty percent of those men who were heading to Vietnam were AWOL or had deserted.

Billy's reprieve lasted only a short time. Within the coming weeks he was offered a deal—a tour of Vietnam to complete his service or several years in the Leavenworth military prison at hard labor. Billy chose Vietnam. By the middle of the summer of 1968 he was in Vietnam on the front lines. Worse was coming.

Bob Russel knew everyone. He was friends with the city's greatest architects, journalists, media tycoons, filmmakers, and TV producers and directors. He lunched with millionaire Bronfmans, Stanfields, and de Gaspé Beaubiens. He wrote policy papers for Liberal and Conservative politicians and top mandarins in Ottawa. One of his greatest supporters was the first of McLuhan's graduate students, currently chair of the Communications Department at McGill. Russel talked often about McLuhan and how he had changed Russel's view of the world.

"Suddenly, I could see how we were in a new cycle that was profoundly and completely changing us and the world. We won't know what's right and wrong about our ideas right now until years in the future. Only future generations will be able to look back on us and see what was important and what wasn't. All the wars and the politics will eventually have to bend to the new world we are creating as we absorb the real changes, changes to the food we eat, to the way we learn, to the way we entertain ourselves and defend our privacy, and handle ourselves in public."

He was applying the same lessons I had learned on the street to the world. The ones most likely to survive were always thinking ten steps ahead and always on the lookout for an opportunity or a wild card or the inevitable joker.

If proof was needed to show how screwed up the world really was, my good-hearted, liberal Republican mother actually began to muse that a solution to the war in Vietnam would be a hybrid Richard Nixon-Eugene McCarthy Presidential ticket. That would put together the two men in the Republican and Democratic parties who were talking most about ending the war. It was a crazy idea but the world was becoming an increasingly crazy and volatile place.

✷ ✷ ✷

Another of my ventures petered out in July. The valiant efforts by Garry's girlfriend to distribute *Take One* in London had amounted to just over a hundred magazines sold. She soon gave up, and Peter Lebensold had to look for a new distributor.

I also had a few more face-to-face talks with John Vader when I went to pick up new assignments. One day, he asked me, "Would you be interested in a new position here as *Midnight's* assistant editor?"

"Yes," I said without hesitation. The contract at Orbafilm still hadn't come through. I was hedging my bets.

Zeke warned me, "John's talking with a few other candidates, some of whom have been freelancing for the tabloids for much longer than you." Some, he said, had newspaper experience at one of Montreal's two English dailies, *The Gazette* and *The Montreal Star*.

I was interested in the job at *Midnight* but still hopeful Orbafilm's contract would come through.

✷ ✷ ✷

After stops in Moscow, Vienna, Budapest, and Jerusalem, Laura left Prague just before the Soviets and other Warsaw Pact members invaded Czechoslovakia, putting an end to the Prague Spring, a period of liberalization the country had experienced since the start of the year.

Due to a postal strike in Canada that lasted a couple of weeks and ended Saturday mail delivery in my new country, half of Laura's letters and cards didn't arrive until after she returned home. When she finally landed in Montreal and called me for the first time, her big news was, "I'm not pregnant." She had missed her period because of nerves brought on by the excitement of her trip.

Both of us were relieved. She definitely wanted to finish school. And I still was trying to get a foothold in my new world. Without a working knowledge of French, I wasn't even sure I could make it for the long haul in Montreal.

I didn't hear anything from John Vader about the new job, so I assumed that I didn't get it. I was okay with that. The promised raise from Russel was coming imminently. I was enjoying the work, and the idea that we were creating the communications platform of the future intrigued me. I was also getting an incredible education from reading newspapers and magazines from around the world and writing and talking constantly about trends, forecasts, and new technologies. Bob, Arthur, and I continued to experiment with ways to write simple, concise, yet punchy abstracts. Down the road, Bob said that Arthur and I could do some of the consulting as our little think tank grew.

"What do you think of this?" I asked Bob one day, pointing to a stack of a half-dozen stories I had just presented to him for his review. Each story promised to solve some problem of the environment, food supply, increasing farm output, social equality, human health, and other conundrums through a new business venture. "If capitalism is responsible for war, then why not find a way to change the model, convince the capitalists that there are more profits in peace than war?"

"We should make that one of our new categories," Bob said with a wave of his hand. Profits from peace. Let's start keywording that into the abstracts."

The future looked exciting.

My mother finally convinced my father to let Jim Rilley, a family friend, drive my mother's station wagon to Montreal instead of taking the bus with my father to visit me. My mother, father, and Jim arrived in Montreal the day Richard Nixon accepted the nomination of his party for President at the Republican Convention in Florida. I had a sick feeling about Nixon, even more so than Johnson, but again my mother found a bright spot in everything. "Nixon was born and raised a Quaker. Quakers are against war." I wanted to believe her so badly that I decided not to think more about it during their visit.

They stayed for nearly a week. I took them to the city's new exhibition park called Man and His World. It had been created from the old Expo '67 buildings. I showed them the Buckminster Fuller Geodesic Dome that had once been the American Pavilion. During Expo the previous summer, American writer and publisher Paul Krassner had burned a fake draft card in front of several US Marines guarding the front of the pavilion. The incident made the national news in Canada and the US.

The highlight of my parents' trip for me was taking them to a theater on St. Catherine Street to see *The Graduate* on the big screen and pointing out all the shots that were supposed to be the UC-Berkeley campus but were really USC's Doheny Memorial Library, the administration building, and the Von KleinSmid Center. The scenes inside and outside of the library were especially meaningful to me because I had worked in the library for two years. I had also watched then-unknowns Dustin Hoffman and Katharine Ross being filmed on the lawn in front of the library in my last semester. The memories were a sad reminder to me of what I had left behind. The loss and sorrow were always present, always filling me with a sense of anxiety as well as a determination to try to do something worthwhile with my life to make up for the self-imposed stigma of ducking the draft.

I say "self-imposed stigma" because aside from several older relatives in the US, no one ever seemed to think I had done the wrong thing. In Canada, being a war resister was a badge of honor to virtually every Canadian I met, with the possible exception of Laura's mother, who thought I was a poor prospect for her daughter. She was right of course. I was Laura's walk on the wild side. Laura was my lifeline to normalcy.

The most disturbing part of my parents' visit was my father. His shaking had almost disappeared. His speech was only a bit slurred, but I saw in his eyes a sense of lost hope, a person who no longer saw much of a future for himself. He told me he thought he might buy a small business he could run himself. He was struggling to stay relevant. I knew my parents didn't have enough money to start a new business. They were struggling to hold onto the house.

That's not me, I told myself with a shiver, knowing that I couldn't escape from the fact that my father was a part of me, maybe my future. He was only fifty-seven. He appeared to be a hundred. The early-onset Parkinson's had been robbing him of his once good health for more than a decade. He was a shell of the handsome, vital man he had been when I was small. I pushed out of my mind any thoughts of being crippled by some disease. He hadn't gotten sick until he was in his mid-forties. I couldn't imagine being that old.

The day after my parents left, I went to work feeling quite confident about my future.

Later that morning, Bob Russel told Arthur and me that the big contract had fallen through. Instead of the raise we were promised, we were both given two weeks' notice.

CHAPTER 19

I WAS WRONG once again. The day after Bob gave me notice—an anxious day, filled with fear and self-doubt—I got a surprise call from John Vader that the job of assistant editor at *Midnight* was mine if I wanted it.

I was in shock. I went to see Vader and accepted the job before I found out what I'd be paid. I was overjoyed to hear that my new salary would be seventy-five dollars a week, thirty dollars more than I'd been making at Orba. For someone who had been living on next to nothing for five years, it was a small fortune.

I was still worried, of course. I was on probation for three months. I had no idea if I could hack the editing work.

I was also thrilled. I would be working in the same bullpen with Zeke during the day. He was getting closer to making his movie with Matt, which meant that if anything broke on that project, I was poised to be in on the ground floor.

✯ ✯ ✯

The elation from my new job that week was profoundly dampened by what happened to my friend Andrew, who had originally introduced me to the poster king. Arty Gold was the one who phoned me. Andrew's lungs had flared up again. When he found out he had inoperable cancer, he had driven himself to the Westmount Summit and shot himself in the head with a handgun.

I felt terrible. In my own whirlwind efforts to find work, make Zeke's movie, and be in love, I hadn't spent much time with Andrew.

"You shouldn't feel guilty," Arty told me. Andrew had practically moved in with Arty and Mary, visiting them every day, listening to records, drinking tea, and talking. "We could see he was getting worse. Even walking a few steps at a time exhausted him, but he continued to insist he was getting better. He knew he was dying. He didn't want to spend his last days in a hospital."

★ ★ ★

In August, I began following more closely and with growing trepidation the news of the Youth International Party (Yippies), founded by Paul Krassner and others, National Mobilization to End the War in Vietnam (The Mobe), Women Strike for Peace, Ralph Abernathy's Poor People's Campaign, Black Panthers, SDS, and other concerned youth converging on Chicago where the Democratic Convention was being held to select the party's candidate for President.

The Democrats were on their way to nominating President Johnson's Vice President, Hubert Humphrey. Humphrey was seen as someone likely to continue Johnson's policies, including the Vietnam War.

On August 23, the Yippies nominated a live pig as their candidate. [16] During the next five days, war protestors and Chicago police repeatedly clashed. The police used batons and tear gas. Many protesters were arrested.

On August 28, an estimated 10,000 to 15,000 protestors attended The Mobe anti-war rally and listened to speeches by Allen Ginsberg, Norman Mailer, Jerry Rubin, Tom Hayden, David Dellinger, and others at the old Grant Park band shell while surrounded by 600 police and in sight of a large contingent of National Guard soldiers.

When news reached the demonstrators outside by radio that the peace plank—which called for an immediate halt to the bombing and withdrawal of troops from Vietnam—had been rejected at the Democratic convention, a young man began to lower a flag flying nearby. Police pushed through the crowd and arrested him, but the flag lowering was completed by others who then held up a bloody shirt as the police moved in again.

The marshals of the demonstration formed a line to protect the protesters from the police, but the police charged, and many were beaten, including activist leader Rennie Davis, who was knocked unconscious.

Demonstrators and police battled in various parts of the city center, culminating in a police riot when the Deputy Police Superintendent ordered police to clear the streets. Demonstrators were clubbed, Maced, beaten with fists, verbally abused, taunted, and arrested. A seventeen-minute attack on demonstrators, and one of the more vicious ones over the convention week, was filmed by TV crews and broadcast across America and around the world to the horror of most Americans—and Canadians. The war had emboldened a large number of young people to go to war against the war.

By the end of the convention week, 668 demonstrators had been arrested. During the same week, more than 300 American soldiers were killed in Vietnam and more than a thousand wounded.

★ ★ ★

My brother sold most of my antique guns to his new friend, my old history teacher, Mr. F., a mercenary in the African wars in the 1950s and a gun dealer on the side. Mr. F. wrote to me saying he bore me no ill will for being in Canada. He did, however, suggest that I return to the US, take the physical, and purposely flunk the psych test, which in his words, would prove I was "mentally unstable." He thought I could do it with my background and degree in psych, and that way, the military would never assign me to anything more than limited duty.

Lie, cheat, do whatever you can to get out of the draft, but don't give up your citizenship in a country that would get into a war like Vietnam in the first place and then not know how to get out of it.

Fuck. Why couldn't everyone see that the war just needed to stop?

The thought of going back to the US was a mental impossibility. The US was not only at war in Vietnam but with itself. I had no interest in fighting anyone.

★ ★ ★

For the time being I still had a choice about where I might be heading next. Billy wasn't as lucky.

My mother wrote in August, a month after Billy landed in Vietnam, that the vehicle he had been riding in had taken a direct hit. He had been wounded in the leg. The soldiers in the vehicle on either side of him had been killed. Within days, Billy had his first Purple Heart and was healed well enough to be sent back to the front lines.

CHAPTER 20

BOB RUSSEL TRIED to hire me back during my first weeks at my new job. One of his much smaller contracts at the Canadian Radio-television and Telecommunications Commission (CRTC) came through. The CRTC was Canada's equivalent of the US Federal Communications Commission. It was headed by Russel's close friend and communications visionary, Pierre Juneau, the former head of the French section of the National Film Board. Russel was helping him to shape policies on Canadian content and new technologies. Collecting newspaper articles for a government agency was more prestigious in my mind than editing *Midnight*, but Russel could only pay me what he had been paying me and he couldn't promise me work for more than a couple of months. In the end, I felt more secure working for a company located in an office building with an elevator and air conditioning. I imagined it would be well heated in the winter.

The Globe Newspaper Group occupied the entire sixth floor. Besides the editorial and art departments in the west wing, the company had an accounting department, offices for circulation staff, an executive suite, and a large boardroom. I had a small benefits package that included hospital coverage.

Outside of the editorial and art departments, the men wore suits and ties and were clean-shaven. The women—almost all of them in secretarial and support roles—dressed up and wore makeup. Many wore high heels.

Except for three nicely dressed, attractive, young secretaries in our section, the editorial and art department employees were men, most of them in their twenties. The guys were about evenly split between junior executives in suits and freaks with long hair, moustaches, and beards.

John became Johnny as soon as I started working full time.

My desk was right outside his door. The window beside me provided a panoramic view of southern Quebec, including three of the Monteregian hills—Saint-Bruno, Saint-Hilaire, and Rougemont. [17] I pretended I could see all the way to the States.

From the start, Johnny was more like a big brother than a boss. I was a fairly competent writer, good enough to make up trashy stories, but I knew nothing about editing a publication. Johnny patiently coached me through the editing processes. He showed me the proofreading marks used to instruct the typesetters and printers. He taught me to write headlines and select typefaces, how to write and position crossheads and captions, and how to arrange a page with just the right balance of text and photos. Whatever else *Midnight* was, the routines needed to lay it out and publish it were like any other professionally printed periodical. I was learning a trade.

On the other hand, creating the content for *Midnight* was anything but conventional.

The cover of each issue was the most important component of the business. *Midnight* had only 5,000 paid annual subscribers who received copies by mail. The majority of the readers—more than a half-million steady readers each week— regularly plunked down their fifteen cents for each issue because they spotted it somewhere and were intrigued by the cover story.

The cover was so important that a good one could attract fifty thousand to two hundred and fifty thousand additional buyers a week, bringing the circulation up to an incredible three quarters of a million readers. The guesstimate was that each issue that someone bought was in turn read by at least one or two other readers, bringing the total readership to well over a million each week.

Sole responsibility for the cover each week rested in the hands of Johnny Vader, The Suit, Zeke, and me. The Suit was one of the junior executives who dressed in expensive business suits and ties as opposed to sloppy hippie garb like the rest of us. The junior executives worked with the editors in various capacities and had small offices in the editorial

wing of our floor or desks in the bullpen. The Suit was the junior executive most involved with John Vader and *Midnight*. He was also Zeke's boss
and said to be well connected to Joe Azaria, who had founded *Midnight* in
the fall of 1954. The Suit had worked for the company since he was a teen-
ager. He had seen it grow into the colossal corporation over the past few
years and was seen by everyone as a possible heir apparent in the empire
or as someone independent and brilliant enough in his own right to
branch off and make a success of himself in another publishing venture
or business.

The editorial cycle for each issue took one working week, starting on
Monday when John, The Suit, Zeke, and I got together to decide on that
week's cover story.

Our main objective was to pick or create something so intriguing that
the casual buyer would stop and say, "Hey, wait a minute. What's *that* all
about?" and then plunk down their money for the paper. We were like
carnival barkers at a sideshow, luring the public into the tent.

While the stories inside each issue ran the gamut from completely fabricated to more or less true, the covers were almost entirely fictitious.
Wildly crazy, made-up, lurid stories—"FBI Uncovers Plot to Steal JFK's
Body," "Government Hushes Up Flying Saucer Murder," and "Man's Nose
Falls Off Every Time He Sneezes"—most often came from the fertile and
seemingly bottomless imagination of Johnny Vader, who had started
working for Joe Azaria during the production of the magazine's third issue.

The Monday morning meeting sometimes ended in twenty minutes
and sometimes ran through lunch, sometimes at a Chinese restaurant
beside the office on St. Catherine Street. The meeting continued until
someone came up with what seemed like a winning headline that the others supported. Although we never formally voted on a cover, it was understood that Johnny's opinion far outweighed the rest of us; The Suit's
was second; and Zeke and I were junior partners in the decision-making
process.

Sometimes a story was fabricated from an actual event. One of the issues that came out just as I started working full time was a takeoff on a
genuine story about an incident in March 1968 in which some 6,000 sheep
mysteriously died on several ranches in Skull Valley, Utah. At the time,

the public wasn't told what had caused the sheep to die. A number of theories floated around. Not until 1998—thirty years after the incident—did the US Army officially admit the sheep had been killed by nerve gas from a test at the Dugway Proving Ground, a US Army chemical and biological warfare testing center base twenty-seven miles away.

Midnight wasn't about to wait thirty years for an answer. After Zeke purchased a legitimate photo of the scene showing ranchers dumping dead sheep onto a pile to be torched, we ran a cover story with the photo and a headline over it in inch-and-a-quarter typeface, screaming: "UFO Kills 6,000 Sheep In Utah."

Like most cover stories, this one was assigned to one of a small group of three or four regular stringers who fleshed out the rest of the story. In this case, the writer wove snippets of facts from legitimate news sources with quotes from fictitious scientists with fancy-sounding, made-up credentials. Our fake scientists and other professionals were often attached to non-existent but legitimate-sounding universities and institutions.

Midnight rarely let truth stand in the way of a good cover as we demonstrated with two other early covers from my first weeks on the job: "Gave Birth When She Was 7 Years Old, Now...GIRL, 15, BECOMES GRANDMA" and "SCIENTISTS BRING 6 MEN BACK FROM DEAD AFTER TWO WEEKS."

I was having a wickedly irreverent time helping to put out the newspaper.

I felt safe and secure for the first time in years. What I didn't understand was the underlying politics of the corporation that would eventually set everything on its head, including me. But that was still months in the future. At the moment, I was happy. I was twenty-three and a new Canadian immigrant. I had an apartment, a job, and enough free time to write, paint, and dream on the side. The only bummers were the war, and Laura and I. We began drifting apart after she returned to university. We never really broke up. We just saw less and less of each other until we stopped sleeping together. By the time of Zeke's party, I was on my own again.

CHAPTER 21

MATT KUNHEIM FINALLY came through with the money to rent a 16 mm camera and tape recorder and buy enough film stock for Zeke so we could start shooting in our spare time.

The money solved only half our problems. As far as I could tell, Zeke had no script or storyline.

"It's a concept, Joseph," Zeke insisted. "It's about sexual obsession and how it runs everything."

It seemed every filmmaker was trying to push the latest boundaries of nudity and sex. His movie was a comedy, he explained, about an ordinary, otherwise likable man, who is obsessed with the scent of women. He becomes so obsessed that he takes to sniffing their bicycle seats to get his fix.

"What's funny about a pervert sniffing bicycle seats?"

"He doesn't think of himself as a pervert but a connoisseur of the ancient habits of humankind when we humans used to smell each other like dogs before we mated. I haven't decided yet whether in the end he gets shot by an irate husband, killed by a mob of women, or escapes with the help of a woman who has fallen madly in love with him."

I wasn't so sure what to think. I kept my mouth shut since I wanted to be part of this budding film group.

For the pervert, Zeke enlisted Herb, a jovial, round-faced designer from the Globe's art department. I had to admit picking someone as likable as Herb for the Sniffer was a brilliant piece of casting.

The night before the first day of shooting, Zeke and Candice threw a party at their apartment.

Zeke told me most of the partygoers were Candice's friends—actors, dancers, and models she worked with. He was hoping to get a few of them to play small parts in his film.

Zeke and Candice's apartment was standing-room-only by the time I got there. I was talking with Matt and his girlfriend, when a striking, tall, olive-complexioned woman with short black hair, high cheekbones, and large brown eyes arrived alone. She was dressed in a white blouse with a yellow miniskirt that showed off her beautiful long legs. She seemed very popular. A dozen people hugged and kissed her as she made her way through the room, stopping on the far side of the room to talk with an actress I knew slightly from one of the Carles' parties. Even in a sea of beautiful people, she stood out. I couldn't keep my eyes off her as Zeke pulled her away from the others and led her to a spot in front of one of the large open windows of the ancient apartment.

I asked Candice who she was while she was still deep in conversation with Zeke.

"That's Alice. She's one of the top models in the city. We're at the same agency. Zeke's hoping to get her for a part in his film. Go over and introduce yourself. I'm sure Zeke wouldn't mind."

I got the feeling Candice was a little miffed. Zeke appeared mesmerized by Alice.

I took my time moving in their direction, finally placing myself in Zeke's line of sight and standing there until he noticed me.

"Joseph, come here. You need to help me convince Alice to be in our movie." He introduced us. "Joseph's a writer from California."

"Ah," she said, eyes lighting up, "A writer. I love writers. What do you write?" Her voice was soft with a hint of an accent.

"I'm working on a screenplay."

"What's it about?" She looked at me with genuine interest.

Before I could tell her, Zeke cut in. "I'm a writer, too, Alice. I wrote our film. Joseph, help me out here. Convince Alice to be in our movie." Zeke was drunk and infatuated with Alice.

He moved several inches closer to her. I half-expected her to back away, but she held her ground as Zeke continued. "It's one of the last taboos that no one wants to talk about. Smell. It's the one thing they haven't been able to duplicate on screen."

"What do you think?" she asked me.

I felt like Zeke; I wanted to make love to Alice.

"It's a concept film," I said, repeating what Zeke had told me. Sensing her uneasiness, I switched subjects and asked her which photographers she liked to work best with in the city, a few of whom I knew through Emile and the Carles.

She seemed pleased that I'd changed the subject. Zeke, Alice, and I ended up talking about favorite films until Alice was dragged off by another couple and Zeke made a beeline for another dark-haired actress he also was hoping to use in his film.

"I hope I'll see you again," I told Alice when she was making the rounds later, saying her goodbyes.

"Will you be working on the film tomorrow?" she asked.

"Yes."

"Then, I might try to stop by." She gave me a nice smile, a hug, and a kiss on each cheek like she did with everyone else before leaving.

In a moment of wishful thinking before I left, I asked Candice whether or not Alice had a boyfriend. "She was going with a writer, but they recently broke up. She loves creative people."

★ ★ ★

The next day I arrived at the designated location down by the docks for our first day of shooting.

Alice wasn't there. Neither was Candice. I heard from one of the other women who had been at the party that Candice and Zeke had a huge fight after I left over Zeke's flirting with another actress.

Zeke was hungover but otherwise in good humor. Matt was there looking more serious than usual. About a dozen others milled around, waiting to get started, including Herb, the art department guy, several other wannabe actors and actresses with bicycles and on foot, and several more people who were there to help with equipment. Zeke was slowly and patiently getting the actors and crew ready to begin shooting as soon as his cameraman figured out how to work the camera and synchronize the tape recorder.

Matt was perturbed because Zeke had only a single page of script describing the morning's shoot.

The scene consisted of showing the Sniffer standing on a street corner, leaning on a telephone pole, watching pedestrians pass by. He ignores everyone, even pretty women, unless one is riding a bike. Then, he follows her with his eyes, waits for her to park her bike. He positions himself near the bike to try to smell the seat when no one is looking, but someone always seems to come by before he can realize his fantasy.

Zeke tried to appease Matt's anxieties by insisting, "This is the establishing scene. Once we get it right and create enough suspense, we'll know exactly what to do next."

Matt was only mildly placated.

Later, while Zeke was busy elsewhere, and I was taking notes—important, Zeke said, for continuity—Matt asked me, "Shouldn't we have a beginning, middle, and end?"

I studiously avoided getting into the argument and simply said, "I think the rest of the script's in Zeke's head."

"But shouldn't he write it down?"

I shrugged. My brain was working overtime to please both Zeke and Matt.

Alice arrived by taxi shortly before we started shooting. She looked even fresher and more dazzling in the morning light than she had the night before. She was dressed in a long, gauzy, summery outfit that was chic, simple, and completely wrong for bicycle riding.

She made it clear to Zeke that she really wasn't interested in being one of the bicycle girls. Zeke was able to coax her into walking along the sidewalk, playing one of the beautiful women on foot. The pervert ignored her because she wasn't on a bicycle.

Alice only stayed for one take and then left for another appointment but not before making a point of giving me a slip of paper with her phone number on it, and telling me, "I really only came because I knew you would be here. Call me later."

✳ ✳ ✳

Excited beyond my wildest expectations, I called her after we finished filming that day. Alice and I ended up having dinner and talking far into the night about everything we had in common. She was well read and a movie fanatic. She was from Northern Italy but had grown up in several different countries in Europe. She came to Canada during a short-lived affair with a Canadian actor. She adored the Beatles.

We fell in love quickly and easily. She began to call me her husband and I started calling her my wife.

Alice had a roommate. We didn't think it was fair to crowd her. So we spent our nights together at my place. Sometimes she'd leave in the middle of the night to return to her apartment to get ready for a job the next morning. She had her own key to my place. She came and went when she felt like it. We began talking about living together and abandoning her apartment as soon as Nicki, her roommate, could find someone to replace her.

When my friends stopped by, Alice told them about our plans to live together and get officially married. Alice was glamorous, gracious, kind, intelligent, well traveled, and well spoken. I felt like the luckiest man alive.

She made me feel like I was interesting, beautiful, and loved. She thought I was a talented writer and brilliant painter. She insisted my gig at *Midnight* was only temporary. She was sure I was on the brink of writing something big. Ideas ran through my head like rivers. She gave me courage and confidence. All she seemed to want from me was my undying love and sex.

I had no doubt that I would write something great. And soon.

Zeke, Matt, and I, and the rest of the itinerant crew continued to film, *The Sniffer*, on weekends in early September on the streets of Old Montreal, Mount Royal Cemetery, and on a vacant lot in Saint-Henri, a dirt-poor working class neighborhood populated mainly by French-Canadians, blacks, and Irish. In Saint-Henri, we not only recruited a couple of members of a local Satan's Choice motorcycle gang to play minor parts chasing the Sniffer, but we staged the final scene—a giant outdoor food fight, complete with cream pies—in which I made my sloppy and uneventful film debut as one of the faces that got creamed.

The film turned out to be a bust on many different levels. Matt and Zeke had a falling out. Matt claimed he owned everything outright because he had put up the money. Zeke thought it was his film. The money wasn't available to finish shooting or editing it.

Matt told me bluntly, "If you want to work with me, you have to work on spec since I'll be paying for the production."

The story that was supposed to materialize from all the disparate scenes, never made any sense to me. It was just a jumble of footage, a rambling, reckless waste of money.

The great surprise for me was to work so closely with the very intellectual and movie-knowledgeable Zeke, who in the end, seemed to have no real sense of how to tell a story. I was also disappointed because my budding film career was already disintegrating.

"Don't worry, darling," Alice told me. She started showing my own rough film treatment to directors and producers she knew.

Whenever Alice and I went downtown together, mainly to look in department stores for new furniture for when she moved in, we ran into other models, actors, photographers, and other beautiful people who knew her and seemed pleased to meet me.

I felt undeservedly proud to see photos of *my girl* in print ads and photos of fashion shows.

I never imagined anything could go wrong.

CHAPTER 22

ZEKE WAS THE first person to try to tell me that Alice was a lot more than a couple of years older than me. More like ten, he insisted. I dismissed his comments as pure jealousy.

Besides, what did it matter? She was ageless. She loved me.

Another friend who had seen me downtown with Alice asked, "Isn't that the model Wally's seeing?"

Wally was a local rich kid who had been in a couple of low-budget movies and was rumored to be writing the great Canadian novel.

"She used to go out with him," I assured my friend. "She's with me now."

I said nothing to Alice. I couldn't ask her something like that. It would show a complete lack of trust.

Then, I dropped by her apartment in Westmount unannounced after work one afternoon. I had done it on numerous occasions before. Sometimes if Alice wasn't there, I'd chat with Nicki for a few minutes before taking off. This time, I intended to deliver a book I had bought Alice. I kept knocking on the door of her apartment because I heard music coming from inside and thought that she or Nicki just might not have heard me. When Alice finally came to the door, she was wearing a dressing gown and an angry frown. She said she was sleeping. She had a headache and was going back to bed. She didn't invite me in. She didn't want the book. I caught a glimpse of Wally framed in the bedroom doorway when he took a quick peek out to see what was going on.

I felt as if I had been fired. I hated her and still loved her. I hated the loss of being invalidated by her as I trudged home alone. A couple of times I thought about returning to her place, but in the end, I felt too humiliated to do more than head home to my empty apartment, play my guitar, and spend the rest of my time telling myself I was better off without her.

It was a lie. I would have done anything to get her back, or at least get back the peace of mind that she brought with her.

A couple of days later, she showed up at my place late at night when I was already in bed. She let herself in with her key. She crawled into bed with me as if nothing had changed, and we made love without saying a word to each other. All the anger that had been swirling around in my head vanished in the heat of the moment.

Afterward, I was afraid to say anything, afraid I would drive her away. I wanted our relationship to be just like it had been. The fantasy was so seductive. She was like warm silk in bed, beautiful to look at. She brought grace into my life.

A few days later, we had a small birthday party for her at my place, just the two of us. She told me she was eight years older than me. I didn't mind.

She assured me I was the only one who mattered in her life. Every cell in my body wanted to believe her, and didn't. I fought against my doubts, knowing that the signals I would send off would drive her away. I felt sad that the virgin honesty between us was gone. Our new life together was grittier, more honestly sexual. I didn't mind.

A couple of days after that, I saw her walking along Crescent Street, clinging to Wally, laughing at something he said, looking at him with the same intensity that I loved so much when she focused all her attention on me. Neither of them noticed me as they passed on the other side of the street. That evening she arrived at my place around ten. I had already made up my mind to say nothing. I quickly broke my promise and told her I'd seen her with Wally. She didn't want to talk. She didn't want to explain. The only thing she said was, "I don't want to see you if you ask so many questions."

We went to bed together. I wanted to believe that everything was all right even after she disappeared in the night while I slept.

She stopped coming by. She wouldn't answer my calls. When I finally got through to Nicki, she told me, "Forget her. She doesn't want to see you."

I ached all over. I had failed in another relationship. I wrote to Sparky and Kaye in California: "Things are working out as usual, not as planned."

I obsessed over ways to win her back. None of them had any chance of succeeding.

Forget it, I told myself.

The only consolation was that the end of the affair sharpened my determination to find what I wanted. I wanted to:

...live a gentle, quiet, ethical, creative life,

...be able to have sex whenever I wanted it,

...be in love with the person I wanted to have sex with,

...have enough money to write, paint, and play music full time,

...write/paint/compose something amazing, something other people would tell their friends to read/look at/listen to, and other writers/painters/musicians would say, I wish I created that,

...I wanted the war to be over.

The funny thing was Alice wanted pretty much what I wanted in her own way, and she was in a much better position to get it. I envied her super powers.

CHAPTER 23

I WASN'T COMPLETELY sure why I couldn't sustain a relationship, but I knew it was, in part, my feelings of being unsettled and incomplete. I threw myself into my work, determined to make a success of something.

Working with Johnny Vader was an absolute delight. He walked me through each new task and always made sure I never had more than I could handle. Soon, we were like partners. When either of us finished a particular job we'd ask the other person if he needed any assistance. It helped that I was eager to try anything. Fortunately, being a very slow but extremely methodical reader made me a fairly good editor. I also wrote features for each issue, the "Letter from the Editor" column, and letters from "From Our Mail" as well as our answers. We never received enough sane or literate letters in a year from readers to fill even one issue of the "From Our Mail" section, so naturally we had to make up our own letters to the editor. I edited copy, wrote headlines and captions, and assigned stories to our stringers. One of my favorite jobs was to create bogus bylines for the articles I edited or wrote. A previous temporary assistant editor had come up with the byline Frank Kafka, a tradition that I carried on. I occasionally slipped in other literary references such as Goethe. On other stories, I used Mark Renzlag—my middle name and an anagram of my last name. Various versions of friends from USC and high school also made it into bylines or into stories as names of fictional protagonists, victims, witnesses, relatives, professionals, or others involved with the mayhem *Midnight* portrayed each week for its sensation-hungry readers.

Best of all, Johnny and I shared the same sense of humor. *Midnight* was raw, edgy, and full of lies, but it was also mainly silly when you came right down to it. From the inside, we were exploring the edge of sanity. We were masters of the "what if?" story.

I told myself I was in the midst of an absurdist's reality, writing satire in a crazy world.

Turning out a weekly tabloid was also hard work. Aside from the writing, editing, and production, it required thinking up or hunting down stories sufficiently enticing each week to hold onto the regulars and capture casual and new readers.

The real trick was inventing a story or a new angle on a story that hadn't already been done. By the time I arrived, some seven hundred issues of *Midnight* with ten to twenty stories a week had already been published. Johnny had been there since the beginning. He had a near photographic memory. He was quick to recognize stories that had already been done when newcomers like Zeke and I proposed them.

We had to come up with a dozen or more new items each week plus literally scores of tidbits on celebrities for the columns, the letters to and from the editor, and other articles.

Midnight was also in a period of transition. From its beginnings in 1954, it had made its mark first in Montreal, then across Canada and North America, selling gore, cheesecake, and the patina of lurid sex, mainly through newsstands on city streets and in bus and train stations.

By the mid-1960s, tastes and demographics were changing. As the suburbs continued to expand, the era of the newsstand began to decline because fewer people took public transportation to work. As the traditional national news distributors to newsstands began to also decline, the *National Enquirer* set up its own distribution business and began successfully pioneering the entry of the tabloids into supermarkets.

Midnight followed right behind the *National Enquirer*, becoming the second tabloid in many instances across North America to appear beside the checkout counters in grocery stores.

I was in on the ground floor as the supermarket tabloid business was born.

Supermarket readers were different from the old newsstand audience. More women than men started buying the tabloids. Women wanted less gore ("MOM CHOPS OFF BABY'S ARMS TO FEED DOG") and male-oriented sexual stories ("GLORIA MARSH Offers $100,000 To Man Who Can Satisfy Her Lust"). Women wanted more titillating stories on celebrities (Mia Farrow, Frank Sinatra, the Kennedys).

The circulation manager, Jack Tabach, a veteran of the early days of *Midnight* like Johnny, was one of the main advocates for change. Jack was largely credited with expanding the circulation across Canada and the US. In the fall of 1968, he was regularly returning to Montreal's head office with stories of supermarkets that had removed issues of *Midnight* from their cash register racks when customers complained about covers that were too violent or sexually explicit. The difficulty was that violent and lurid covers were still selling well in the traditional newsstand settings but not in the supermarkets. So we had to try to keep the old readers happy while simultaneously building a new readership by switching back and forth between the old cruder stories and the new softer, celebrity-oriented gossip.

I was welcomed as a new ideas man. I came up with scores of new ideas, but I soon found that most of my seemingly brilliant ideas had already been done. I bided my time, certain that I would come up with something that no one had ever done.

One of the changes to the content right after I joined was the addition of predictions from a new *Midnight* psychic. Astrologer and psychic Jeane Dixon was all the rage at the time. She was still riding high on her fame from her *Parade* magazine prediction in 1956 where she said that a Democrat would be elected in 1960 and he would be assassinated in office. Never mind that she predicted four years later in 1960 that Nixon would actually win that year's election. Once President Kennedy had been gunned down in Dallas in 1963, her credibility soared. Buying rights to her predictions became increasingly expensive. So Johnny came up with the idea to create *Midnight's* own psychic. The perfect person to write the predictions was a large, older woman named Mrs. D. She had been freelancing for *Midnight* for several years, writing articles as well as the "Your Horoscope" column. Anyone who actually read and believed her very popular horoscope column would be shocked to know that Mrs. D. simply turned in twelve fortune-cookie-like paragraphs of predictions each week, and after they were edited and typeset, the art department simply cut up the proofs and pasted her predictions randomly under Pisces or

Aries or one of the other signs of the zodiac. Anyone who read all the predictions each week—not just their own or one or two others—would have seen a lot of duplication as the same prediction for one astrological sign was often recycled under another sign a few weeks or months later.

Our new psychic was to be a numerologist, as well as astrologer and psychic, in part because numerology was in vogue. More important, it took absolutely zero imagination to invent someone's lucky number, unlucky number, or favorable day. I came up with the idea for an additional number—a personal Life Cycle Vibration Number, which in turn spawned a Life Cycle Vibration Number profile and an individual personal symbol based on your personal number.

To my delight, Johnny let me choose the name of our new psychic and create her biography. I dubbed her Madame Yolanda Savarini—a completely fabricated name that sounded exotic to me. She soon became the new face of the astrology column with her own personal history, which I created. I gave her credit for predicting Bobby Kennedy's assassination, the outcome of the most recent Arab-Israeli conflict, and the beginning of the US-North Vietnam peace talks in Paris. She was, according to me, the director of the august-sounding Institute of Applied Astrology and Numerology in London, the author of several acclaimed textbooks on the paranormal, and a consultant to influential financiers, statesmen, and others—all invented by me.

To complete our imaginary seer, we turned to the art department to conjure up a photo. Although *Midnight* regularly purchased photos of celebrities and others from legitimate news outlets, the tabloids also needed a steady stream of stock photos, especially to depict made-up characters in our invented stories. Over the years, the art department had been collecting boxes of old photos, many from old folks' homes from the liquidated possessions of elderly people who died without heirs. These and other, often unidentified photos, which found their way to the art department, became the source for photos of fake people in our stories—from victims of crimes and so-called esteemed professors and authorities in their fields to criminals and others who populated the pages of the tabloids. The photo of Madame Savarini came from one of these boxes. Our Madame Savarini was a kind-looking, white-haired woman with large, sympathetic-but-serious eyes, and a thoughtful expression. Through the power of tabloid make-believe, I had resurrected a forgotten old woman, whose life had ended anonymously in some old folks' home, into a glamorous and vital human being who could predict the future. I had helped create, in a sense, a geriatric superhero.

During the transition period, as the paper began to reach gradually beyond sex, gore, and the paranormal, Johnny began experimenting in different directions, several of which turned into real flops. One blatant failure was a jab at the Pope's infallibility with a cover headline that proclaimed: "The Pope Is Wrong." The issue bombed. Similarly, Johnny ran across a legitimate story, which told how the hands of black workers in certain chemical plants had turned white. He created a cover that said, "Ointment Turns Black People White." It, too, resulted in a very serious drop in sales, mainly, Johnny theorized afterward, because blacks didn't want to turn white.

One of the areas generally shunned was politics, but during this period of experimentation, Johnny was open to trying anything that might boost sales. As a result, a few weeks after I arrived, he ran a cover that said: "In First Interview Since Assassination Sirhan's Dad Tells...WHY MY SON KILLED BOBBY KENNEDY."

Taken from alleged quotes from Sirhan's father, Sirhan Bishara, a rabidly anti-Zionist Christian Palestinian, it was filled with anti-Israeli diatribes and speculation on how his son, a fanatic Arab nationalist, thought Bobby Kennedy would be bad for the Arab world. In short, Bobby's assassination was a revenge killing.

Although the issue didn't sell that well, we continued to experiment, which opened the door for me to invent still another story about political assassination.

I still harbored a fondness for Paul Krassner and *The Realist*, and continued to want to believe that *Midnight* was in some way a kissing cousin of Krassner's politically hip, often vulgarly satirical underground paper. So, I began pushing a story that I believed could sell papers. It came from my disdain for all three Presidential candidates running in the election in 1968—Richard Nixon, Hubert Humphrey, and George Wallace. It also appealed to my sense of "what if"—what if Nixon won but was assassinated before he took office? Assassination was still on everyone's mind. We were only a few months past the assassinations of Martin Luther King, Jr. and Senator Robert Kennedy.

Richard Nixon was running, in part, on the premise that he had a "secret plan" to end the War in Vietnam. My mother and millions of Americans believed him. I was skeptical, but it nevertheless made him an ideal target for an assassination attempt by the far right. Alleged far right conspirators, including men with CIA connections and Cuban and Latin connections, were being hotly pursued by New Orleans District Attorney Jim Garrison, who for the last two years had been investigating a cabal of men who were said to be the real assassins of President Kennedy. Garrison believed JFK was killed because he had failed to support an invasion of Cuba and was getting cold feet in Vietnam. Garrison would soon bring several of these men to trial, providing new fodder for many future issues of *Midnight*.

My proposed headline was simple: "FBI Uncovers...PLOT TO KILL NIXON."

In my mind's eye, I was a grand film producer like Cecil B. De Mille creating a blockbuster. I never liked Nixon, and it wouldn't have surprised me if he had been involved in a murky conspiracy to kill Kennedy. In a bizarre twist of fate, Nixon had actually been in Dallas on the morning that President Kennedy had been assassinated.

Zeke, who saw himself as a Canadian leftist idealist, was as keen as I was to produce my story. The Suit deferred to Johnny. Johnny made the final decision with a shrug, and we were off and running on the next cover story by late Monday morning, October 14, 1968, three weeks before the '68 Presidential election. The dates related to the creation and publication of this story turned out to be important.

Johnny let me produce the story by myself. I picked the stringer and hammered out a general outline with him.

A recent confrontation between Mexico and the US regarding the border had been in the news. So I suggested some Mexican assassins be brought into the mix. The assassination attempt was to take place in New York where Nixon lived and where I conveniently put him in an imaginary convertible during an imaginary campaign parade before the election.

I decided we needed some photos of FBI agents holding rifles confiscated from the would-be assassins. Zeke thought it would be easier to create the photo than to buy one. The next day, Zeke and I arranged for a
photographer to take pictures of us at a local sporting goods store on St.
Catherine Street each holding a hunting rifle and a handgun. The idea
was to run black slashes across our eyes, so our identities wouldn't be
compromised, and then run a caption below saying, "Unidentified FBI
agents with confiscated weapons."

The stringer finished the story on Wednesday afternoon. Johnny and
I both edited it.

The original story called for the arrest of three conspirators near
Nixon's townhouse. Since the story was bogus we decided to leave as
much as possible to the imagination. The two captured conspirators were
simply said to be in an American jail, while a co-conspirator was in a Ti-
juana jail.

The only disappointment for me was that we decided to substitute a
photo of the assassination of Bobby Kennedy for the one of Zeke and me
holding the guns. Little did I know that this seemingly inconsequential
omission turned out to be a lucky break.

CHAPTER 24

THE COPY FOR my first cover story—"FBI Uncovers...PLOT TO KILL NIXON"—went to the printer to be typeset. The proofs were sent back, corrected, and laid out with the photos and other art work and sent back and forth during the following week until the finished paper was ready to go to press on Friday night, October 25.

Johnny took me to the plant on Friday night, something that he normally did alone. I went because this was my first cover story. He thought I'd like to see the complete operation.

I watched Johnny take a last look at the proofs from the blueprints. The paper was just beginning its run on the huge presses of Pierre Péladeau's giant printing company, Quebecor. Johnny still had time to pull the plug if he found something wrong on our latest issue. "I'm only looking for major errors, like the date, which could affect the accounting system," he explained.

After a quick, practiced glance, once with his glasses on, once squinting with them off and the paper held close to his face, he gave the okay for the full run to begin.

I was thrilled to see my first cover story in print. Inside, the lead story boasted: "Plot to Assassinate Nixon Is Nipped in the Bud."

The date on the masthead for the issue was November 4, 1968. It would take that long for the full print run to be completed and shipped over the border to regional hubs before finally being distributed locally in cities and suburbs across the US.

Canadian issues appeared on newsstands a week earlier, October 28, with the November 4 date on the masthead. I bought copies at a half-dozen newsstands and mom-and-pop corner stores on the way home so I could ask the cashier how it was selling. The answer was the same, "Not so bad, but nothing like the stories about movie stars."

Not a homerun but also not a complete failure.

By the end of the week, we were putting to bed another issue. The only thing left to do was wait for the circulation figures to see how my cover affected sales in the States.

If my cover increased sales, I would be hailed as a minor boy genius. If they decreased, I might get fired. I was still on probation.

Our paper, as planned, hit the streets of New York City and the rest of America on Monday, November 4.

On November 5—the day of the US Presidential election—at 7:30 p.m. a New York City policeman arrested a gun-toting foreigner—an Egyptian, Edward Hotter, 30—five blocks from Nixon's townhouse at 810 Fifth Avenue. Hotter was nabbed carrying a .22 rifle by a patrolman guarding the Yugoslav Mission to the UN. [18]

Four days later, Yemeni immigrants, Ahmed Namer and his two sons, were arrested in their Brooklyn apartment for allegedly conspiring to assassinate Nixon after Ahmed, an alleged former spy in Yemen and a naturalized US citizen, had attempted to recruit an acquaintance to help. The acquaintance instead reported them to the authorities, who also found two rifles and ammunition at the apartment of the alleged conspirators. [19]

Over the next several days the real arrest stories were widely covered by most of the mainstream press. My *Midnight* story got caught in the FBI's radar. Johnny told me the Royal Canadian Mounted Police came to the Globe's offices and made inquiries on behalf of the FBI.

Johnny was interviewed by the Mounties. He said the head of the accounting department was also interviewed. Johnny's defense was that the newspaper had an obligation to protect its sources. Johnny, a kid at heart, saw the whole incident as great fun.

Johnny told me the head of the accounting department was not happy. I could have created a nightmare for the company. I cringed at the thought that my photo might have been part of the article.

The official inquiry into *Midnight's* story seemed to blow over quickly, but I continued to wonder from time to time whether my name had ever been associated with the story by the RCMP or the FBI. As usual, the by-line on the story was one of our fake ones. The stringer was one of our regulars who had no interest in becoming more deeply involved.

When the numbers came in from the circulation department, the Nixon-assassination-attempt issue did so-so—about on par with the cover story reporting the sheep killed in Utah by the UFO, which had been published a couple of months previously.

I thought I would be chastised for my bad judgment, but the low numbers for one issue barely rated a mention from Johnny or anyone else.

"Always be looking ahead," Johnny told me.

Besides, by then, something had happened that literally would add jet fuel to the supermarket side of the tabloid business.

Between the time we started the Nixon cover and the time it hit the streets, one of the most shocking human interest stories of the 1960s took place. On October 20, 1968 President Kennedy's widow, Jacqueline Bouvier Kennedy, married the short, bug-eyed, richer-than-Midas, mogul-of-moguls, Aristotle Onassis.

The marriage to Onassis became instant and constant fodder for not only *Midnight* but tabloids and mainstream newspapers around the world.

Emotions ran high when it came to the marriage. Many Americans felt jilted and betrayed when Jackie, a symbol of youth, vitality, and American royalty, married a foreigner and someone twenty-three years her senior with a reputation as a playboy.

Midnight soon developed its own lurid angle on the Jackie wedding with two stories purported to be interviews with Onassis's longtime, now-spurned girlfriend, opera superstar Maria Callas, and Jackie's rumored secret lover, Lord Harlech. Maria Callas called Jackie "a love thief" and said that although Jackie was feminine and alluring on the outside, not only did she lack a heart and a soul, but inside she was nothing but "a frozen mackerel." As for the fifth Lord Harlech, David Ormsby-Gore, he was painted as a bitter ex-suitor, complaining that he had offered Jackie love but she only wanted to "swing."

Even before *Midnight's* first "Jackie" issue after the Onassis marriage had been put to bed, Johnny caught the wave and produced a sequel to the first, with a headline screaming: "WHY SHE WED ONASSIS...Leading Psychiatrist Declares: JACKIE IS MENTALLY SICK...BOBBY'S DEATH CAUSED 3RD NERVOUS BREAKDOWN."

To give the story more credibility, *Midnight* ran a shot of a previous "Jackie" cover published on January 8, 1968 that said, "Famous Psychiatrist Says: JACKIE IS ON VERGE OF NERVOUS BREAKDOWN."

Like the first "breakdown" story, the second one was completely fabricated. The psychiatrist was made up.

Circulation of the "Jackie" issues shot through the roof.

We got the message loud and clear. Jackie sold newspapers. Other Jackie covers quickly followed. The last issue of 1968 was an alleged interview with a sailor on Onassis's yacht, who revealed, "JACKIE'S HONEYMOON WAS A FLOP..."—because she locked Onassis out of her bedroom.

The story ran alongside articles about Ava Gardner telling how she became great in bed; why licorice can kill you; a jilted lover who mailed a bomb that blew a rival to bits; Marlon Brando's VD; a topless salesgirl in Copenhagen who sold porn, and a man's brain kept working by a flashlight battery.

A week later, we were back with *Midnight's* annual predictions of the coming year, this time by the newly anointed "famed" astrologer Madame Savarini. She foretold that Jackie—pursued by the "evil" astrological star that had haunted her since her marriage—would have a deformed baby over the coming year.

Madame Savarini didn't have much good to say about 1969 in general. Johnny and I and another writer, who contributed to the forecast, were filled with doom and gloom, predicting a VD epidemic for the US, a collapse of the monetary system, and a new Great Depression. We also predicted America would be confronting a different kind of ghetto warfare in US cities led by highly trained and armed combat vets returning from Vietnam. We forecast a nervous breakdown for Mia Farrow, a new bride for Frank Sinatra (but the marriage would crumble almost immediately), a secret Russian weapon that would give the Arabs a leg up in a new Middle East conflict, and the resignation of Senator Ted Kennedy, who would focus more on trying to find the real killers of President Kennedy in partnership with Jim Garrison. Garrison, we predicted, would be the target of a campaign orchestrated from high places to make it appear he was mentally ill. Madame Savarini also forecast a disastrous fallout with a friendly power through a Nixon blunder that would result in an attempt to impose a steering committee presidency by Republican leaders, and a break between the US Catholic Church and the Roman Catholic Church over the pill and marriage for priests and nuns. At the top of my own wish list, our sage predicted that the South Vietnamese government would betray the US and make a secret deal with the Communists and Viet Cong, and work out their own problems without American troops. Equally startling, Madame Savarini predicted astronauts would make contact with space aliens who were using the dark side of the moon as a base for observing earth, but the US and Russia would enter into an agreement to censor the information to prevent widespread panic.

What Madame Savarini never mentioned was her own impending doom, which had been unfolding right before the eyes of *Midnight's* loyal followers for weeks.

Never mind that Madame Yolanda Savarini was one of the worst forecasters in the annals of astrology. Her undoing began a few weeks after we initially launched her in the early fall of 1968. One morning, Manfred, *Midnight's* layout man, informed Johnny and me that the original photo of Madame Savarini had been misplaced.

For weeks, then months, we kept hoping it would turn up. In the meantime, the only way to reproduce Madame Savarini's image was from the printed image in the newspaper, resulting in a very low-grade reproduction. It made our seer look very washed out.

With no chance of ever finding another photo of the same woman, I was convinced Madame Savarini was doomed if her original photo didn't surface.

Johnny just laughed it off. In the end, we simply found a photo of another elderly, white-haired, forgotten old woman and substituted the new photo for the fading one. "No one is likely to notice," Johnny assured me, "and if they do, they won't care."

Sure enough, the new face of Madame Savarini simply took over from the old one without a hitch, and our seer continued to spout her false wisdom for years to come. At the time, it never occurred to me that my own career at *Midnight* might be as precarious as our original seer's.

CHAPTER 25

MOM WROTE TELLING me that Dad had to have all his teeth pulled. He continued to have trouble with his speech. I suggested he try singing. He did, and it helped.

My mother was sure Nixon would be good for the country. As a Quaker, he was a pacifist at heart, she repeated. She still believed in his still-unrevealed secret plan to end the war. Although the Democrats still controlled Congress, everyone had been voted in on their peace promises.

The FBI also made their first visit to my parents' house in New Jersey in mid-November 1968.

My father, who was spending most of his time alone at the house because he couldn't drive very far, was happy for company. He invited the federal investigator inside and chatted with him for an hour. My FBI agent said I could return to the States any time. I was in no real trouble yet, but I would have to serve in the military.

"He knows where you are," my mother told me, when she phoned that evening.

Of course, he knew where I was. I had sent my draft board a letter with my new address on St. Urbain Street shortly after I moved in.

But what else did he know?

The first visit from the FBI agent assigned to me was a few weeks after the Nixon-attempted-assassination story. The timing of the visit made me wonder if the FBI had connected me to that.

His visit also reminded me yet again that I was a criminal in the US, and the border was only forty miles from where I lived.

I continued to try to mentally and physically adjust to my new home.

"I miss the ocean in California but the winter in Canada is what I am learning from now. It is so pure and white that it doesn't leave me time to think about being bigger than some other cat or stronger or different," I wrote to my mother, wondering what the FBI thought of that if they read it.

Eloise, a French-Canadian freelance writer from a small town on the other side of the border in Ontario, showed up one day at the *Midnight* offices and became one of Johnny's favorite new regulars. Eloise and I ran into each other a few times in clubs on Crescent Street and began to see more of each other. We were two writers, trying to stay alive while we dreamed of writing our novels and movies. Eloise was full of energy, intelligent, funny, and adventurous in bed. We spent half our time in her rented room on Hutchison Street and half at my place. We were in love with no commitments, two soldiers of fortune working our way through the writing world. Montreal wasn't her final destination. She was just passing through, picking up extra money writing for *Midnight* before heading to Paris.

She had a friend in the apartment beside her who liked to get high every night and had a record player. The friend bought *The Beatles* album—aka *The White Album*. Eloise and I went there and listened to it a few times. We were a little disappointed in it. I personally didn't get the same buzz I got off of the *Sgt. Pepper's* album at the beginning of the Summer of Love a year and a half before. Even the *Magical Mystery Tour* album had songs that grabbed me, like "Strawberry Fields Forever," "Penny Lane," "Magical Mystery Tour," and "All You Need Is Love."

The only welcome surprise for me on *The White Album* was "While My Guitar Gently Weeps," by George Harrison. George was the closest in age to us.

"Blame Yoko," Eloise's friend joked.

None of us liked the *Two Virgins* album, which came out three weeks after John and Yoko were busted for marijuana. For me, disliking the *Two Virgins* had nothing to do with how I felt about Yoko. In truth, I didn't think of her very much, or of John Lennon, for that matter. Their personal lives had nothing to do with me. All I could say about any music was whether I liked it or not. For me, the *Two Virgins* just wasn't pleasant or exciting or seductive. Maybe it was to John and Yoko, and that was okay. They had the right to do what they wanted. [20]

"George is probably the Beatle I'd most want to get high with," Eloise told me, "but John would be the most fun to go with to crash a party."

Eloise wasn't madly in love with me. I wasn't madly in love with her. I was having trouble thinking about permanence, but we got along well, and if I had been free to travel, I might have picked up stakes and gone with her to Paris. We talked about me coming to see her once she got settled, but I don't think either of us believed it.

She left Montreal as planned a few weeks before Christmas. A few months after that, I got a postcard from her from Paris with no return address.

CHAPTER 26

ZEKE'S DISLIKE OF *Midnight* continued to grow. He thought the job was sleazy and beneath him. He was dying to break into film or TV. He had been pursuing leads on real news stories on the side whenever possible. He relentlessly followed the conventional news and pitched the TV and radio news bureaus of the CBC on new angles for stories that he thought they should be covering but weren't.

Zeke began to spend less of his time at the office to the chagrin of The Suit.

Zeke was only one of The Suit's distractions. The Suit liked to bet heavily on sports, sometimes as much as a thousand dollars on a single game. He spent a great deal of his time analyzing various teams and players. Luckily, he could do his job with his eyes closed even when Zeke wasn't around. Zeke was out of the office more than half the time, ostensibly hunting for stories but in reality seeing movies, going to political rallies, and hanging around the bars on Crescent Street and in Old Montreal, looking for people interested in investing in films.

I sometimes tagged along on a slow workday when it didn't interfere with my job.

One afternoon, Zeke told me, "Joseph, I have to tell you something important. But you have to promise you won't tell anyone."

I promised.

"I met a New York producer who's putting together a feature film right here in Montreal. He's offered me a job. I can come to work for him now on spec until they get their financing. I said I would do it. I'm just keeping the job with the Globe to get a paycheck. The producer of the film already has a verbal agreement with a major Hollywood Studio and the contract is working its way through their legal people."

Zeke was more excited than I'd ever seen him. But after my experiences with the poster king and Orbafilm, I was wary of fly-by-night ventures.

"How big is the company you're working for?"

"Right now, it consists of the producer, the director, and me in a loft on St. Lawrence Boulevard." The address was only a few blocks from my apartment.

"I'm the associate producer," he said with pride. "As soon as the deal closes, we go right into production and start hiring."

"Do you need a writer?"

"We have to use someone with film credits, but I'll introduce you to the producer. He's from New York. He's got a million ideas, and he's open to everything."

Over the next few weeks, Zeke showed up just enough at the office to keep from getting fired.

✲ ✲ ✲

I pondered quitting when I thought too long and hard about some of the stories we were turning out. While Zeke had been there almost a year, I had been working there only a few months. I needed to stick it out for the time being. I didn't have another job to go to or a working wife paying the living expenses like Zeke did. I also knew I wasn't a lifer like Johnny. The main reason I kept going was that I left the US telling myself I could make it as a writer. Even writing and editing *Midnight* was teaching me something, and I was writing in English.

✲ ✲ ✲

The December 1968 issue of *Esquire* added to the legitimacy of the strange world I worked in. The magazine ran a story titled "Captain Midnight" by Robert H. Williams on Joe Azaria, founder and sole owner of *Midnight*. The story, which sang praises about Joe and his empire, was sandwiched in with Susan Sontag's "Trip to Hanoi," Norman Mailer's "At Play in the Fields of the Bored," and "Brooklyn is" by James Agee.

I felt almost legitimate. [21]

CHAPTER 27

BY THE TIME The Globe Newspaper Group Christmas party rolled around shortly before the holidays at the end of 1968, everyone knew Joe Azaria had new plans to expand the organization. He was planning to buy *The National Police Gazette*, a US true crime magazine that had been around since 1845. More interesting, he planned to start a new Montreal English-language newspaper, the *Sunday Express*. It was to be a working class tabloid-style weekly, heavy on sports, entertainment, and local news. Montreal had two English-language newspapers, *The Gazette*, a thin but respected newspaper without a Sunday edition, and *The Montreal Star*, the dominant newspaper with a Sunday edition. Joe's idea was to provide an alternative to the *Star's* Sunday edition. Once his Sunday edition was successful, he planned to go daily.

The Globe Newspaper Group at that time employed around forty to fifty people, including the administration and circulation departments, so everyone more or less knew everyone's face and name. The largest meeting I ever attended was the regular Monday cover-story sessions with John, The Suit, Zeke, and me. There were no department or company-wide meetings. Joe, who once micromanaged every aspect of the newspaper and even wrote most of the features in the early years, no longer even ventured into the editorial or art departments.

Nevertheless, Joe knew who I was, in part, because I ran into him periodically at lunchtime when I went out with Johnny. Johnny took great delight in introducing us as "Joe meet Joe" even though everyone else called me Joseph. I knew Johnny was doing me a favor, opening a casual door to the boss and giving him a way to remember me.

A week or so after one of my introductions to Joe, he had asked me how I liked working there, and I said I was enjoying it. "Good." He smiled and hurried down the hallway in the other direction.

When I saw Joe Azaria standing alone halfway through the Friday evening Christmas party in the conference room I decided to wish him a personal happy holidays. Joe was a small, slim, well-dressed man with large, hooded, dark eyes. I was flattered that he remembered my name. I mentioned how impressed I was with the *Esquire* magazine article. To think, I said, he had started the newspaper when he was only twenty-five-years old, two years older than me. We started talking about success in general, and he told me that one of the ways he got so much done was that after he went to sleep, no matter what time he woke, he never went back to sleep but pulled himself out of bed and worked on something even if it was three or four in the morning.

I told him I often got up at three or four in the morning. I had been doing it since high school. I loved the solitude of the early morning and seeing the dawn and the new day emerge from the blackness. It gave me a sense that I had a jump on the day.

He was curious about what I had written before *Midnight.* I told him about my firsthand account of the Los Angeles Watts Riots of 1965, my unpublished novel, the workbook I had written for *Psychology and Life,* and my stint at Bob Russel's think tank.

When I mentioned I was working on a film script on the side, he said, "Why don't you try writing film reviews for the new newspaper?"

It was a startling proposal. I immediately said yes.

Over a handshake, I became the *Sunday Express's* almost-first-ever movie critic with the emphasis on "almost."

✷ ✷ ✷

In addition to my day job editing *Midnight,* I threw myself into my new assignment as film critic. After work, I haunted the movie theaters, seeing every first-run English-language movie in town, sometimes sitting through a movie twice, making notes, trying to scribble down the names of the actors, the director, and writer from the credits, and trying to figure out how to write a review. No one told me I could go to the distributor and get a press package. I tried to take everything from the screen.

Worse, after scrutinizing and talking endlessly about movies for the past several years, I realized I hadn't a clue how to write a review.

For once, even my ability to mimic other writers failed me. I read the movie reviews in *The Gazette, The Montreal Star,* and *Take One.* I spent hours typing up essays on the movies, trying to make my writing sound authoritative and interesting like the reviews I read. Though I could tell if I liked or didn't like a movie, I just didn't have the lingo or enough film history under my belt to write what I thought would be a credible and intelligent review.

Still, I kept going to movies and coming home to pound out page after page of commentary late into the night. When I read what I wrote the next morning, it inevitably sounded trite.

After struggling for a couple of weeks, I finally had to admit that I hadn't turned out one credible movie review. I had utterly failed. Rather than just fade away without a word, I headed down the hall and popped in on Joe.

He greeted me like an old friend and seemed unfazed about my failure. "Don't worry about it. Johnny tells me you're a good writer. Maybe you should try writing a feature for the new newspaper. When you're ready, tell Colin to give you a try."

★ ★ ★

Colin was Colin Gravenor. Colin had been a public relations man for local and visiting celebrities and bluebloods in Montreal. He had also been a part-time writer and editor in the early days of *Midnight* while he dabbled in real estate. He had made his first fortune in real estate, hitting the jackpot in the mid-1950s, and becoming a millionaire as a middleman who had turned Nuns' Island, a near useless, windswept island in the St. Lawrence River, into one of Montreal's trendiest new suburbs. He had now rejoined Joe as managing editor of the *Sunday Express.*

I was flattered that Johnny said nice things about me to Joe, and even more flattered that Joe wanted to give me a try elsewhere in his organization.

I was also not quite ready to take another plunge so soon after my most recent false start. I felt chastened. I decided to bide my time before approaching Colin Gravenor.

CHAPTER 28

My MOTHER WAS finding escape in her art. She had started to draw flowers again. She had been a successful fashion sketcher and designer on Seventh Avenue in New York during the Depression but had rarely drawn or painted since she quit the business when she became pregnant with my older brother. She was now toying with the idea of drawing other people's houses. "People are so vain about their houses," she wrote. She wasn't dreaming of being famous, just imagining what it would be like to be able to make a little extra money on the side to supplement her two part-time jobs.

My poor, struggling father was learning how to add and subtract again, and his memory was improving.

Another great uncle—he had been a socialist, maybe even a Communist during the Depression before he went into business and made millions in medical supplies—surprised everyone in the family when he told my mother that he approved of me going to Canada. His son had a deferment for medical school. Vietnam was turning out to be the most unpopular, most avoided war of the century for men of draft age.

My mother was very impressed with Joe Azaria when she read the *Esquire* article. "He's someone you can learn from." Education had always been the greatest god in our family.

★ ★ ★

Family friend Billy was still on the front lines in Vietnam. He was wounded badly enough a second time to get another Purple Heart but not enough to be sent home or even to the rear. The medics patched him up and sent him right back into combat.

As the old year ended, and the New Year began, I reflected on how much my life had changed. In a year, I had gone from stateless to working as a writer and editor in a corporation with an international reach. I had landed more or less on my feet after stints with the poster king, Bob Russel's think tank, Zeke's first movie experience, and the corporate environment of the Globe. Even after the assassinations of Martin Luther King Jr. and Senator Kennedy and the election of President Nixon, I still felt a great hunger for news of the old country and a deep nostalgia for everyone and everything I had left behind. I had also had my eyes opened to Canada and the rest of the world, and to America in a way that could never have happened if I had remained in the US. The secret of happiness, I told myself, was being happy with what you have, not what you imagine you deserve.

CHAPTER 29

EARLY IN THE New Year, 1969, Johnny introduced me to his stockbroker who visited him regularly at the office. The stockbroker told me about a half-dozen investment opportunities. I wanted to fit in with corporate Canada. The idea that the small grubstake I had put together to finance my next shot at writing full time might grow much faster in stocks than a savings account intrigued me. I quickly became the proud investor of $200 in shares—about three weeks' net salary and several months' savings—in a new nickel and bismuth mine in the Northwest Territories. I understood nothing the broker told me except that it was a very good deal and I was in on the ground floor.

Later, I invested the rest of my savings—a thousand dollars—in mutual funds. I was so enthusiastic about this that I wrote home to my mother and told her, "With the economy the way it is at the present time, this is the only way for the individual to make a substantial outside income above and beyond a steady salary." The mutual fund I was investing in was a sure thing. Called Investors Overseas Services, its funds operated in Canada but were run out of Switzerland by an American named Bernie Cornfeld, who had been called a financial genius by many of the most-respected business publications I had abstracted at Orbafilm.

My money was safe. I was safe. My venture into the stock market was one more sign that I had survived my exit from the US and established a toenail hold in a new country.

By the end of January 1969, I was feeling confident enough to take up Joe Azaria's suggestion and ask Colin Gravenor for an assignment at the *Sunday Express.*

CHAPTER 30

REAL ESTATE TYCOON and public relations genius Colin Gravenor had commandeered an empty desk at the back of our editorial bullpen.

After Colin arrived, a steady stream of new faces showed up almost daily. Some came and went after brief conversations with Colin. Others took over empty offices and nearby desks.

Colin was a few months shy of his fifty-ninth birthday, a year older than my ailing father.

By the time I crossed paths with Colin, he was on his second wife and second set of children. He was living in a large home on Grosvenor Avenue on the hill in Westmount, the premier neighborhood in the downtown.

Colin Gravenor was still riding high from his earlier real estate successes but looking for a new adventure. The job of managing editor of the *Sunday Express* for Joe Azaria was perfect.

I watched him throw himself into the job with great gusto. When he wasn't on the phone and scribbling notes or talking with someone sitting in the chair beside his desk, he was pounding away at his manual upright typewriter, churning out stories.

Like a linebacker who had gone somewhat soft around the waist in middle age but nevertheless still had the game in his blood, Colin was both a father figure and an intimidating warrior with thick eyebrows over small, narrow, piercing eyes, and a small moustache over an equally small mouth set in a square, jowly, determined jaw.

I was fascinated by him, just as I was by Joe Azaria. I never saw myself becoming like them, but I was still captivated by their energy. They used their wits, attracted others to them, and took enormous risks beyond anything I could imagine. They both became successful and wealthy as much by their own energies as their ability to attract others to their ventures. I wanted to be a part of their worlds if for no other reason than to see how these men operated.

I kept looking for a story to bring to Colin.

One of the big stories affecting downtown Montreal during January 1969 was the student protest at Sir George Williams University, a block north of our office. [22]

I gathered background information, hoping I might find an angle that wasn't being covered by the two English-language dailies. I sourced my information through friends attending the university, like Arty Gold, who was taking poetry classes there from George Bowering. I intended to get the views of a couple of the administrators of the university as well once I got the go-ahead from Colin to write the story.

The students were protesting against racism at the school after several black students accused their biology professor of giving them lower marks than they should have received because they were black. The recriminations led to months of small protests and negotiations as students and local radicals made the complaints public and tried to get a Hearing Committee formed with student and administration representatives and the professor to address the charges.

When the Hearing Committee was established, the students didn't feel it was really representative, and by January 29, 1969, about two hundred students and local radicals walked out of the hearings and occupied the university's Computer Center.

One of the novelties of the university was that it was so self-contained. The entire university was housed in a single ten-story building that took up an entire square block of downtown. The computer department was on the ninth floor of the three-year-old modern, cube-style Henry F. Hall Building.

Negotiations between the students and the administration seemed to be going well after eleven days. An agreement was in the works between the administration and the students to end the sit-in in exchange for amnesty for the students and help for those who had missed course work due to the hearings and demonstrations. About half of the student and non-student demonstrators left the building late in the afternoon of February 10, believing the deal had been accepted by the administration. When the remaining demonstrators learned that negotiations had broken down later that night, they blocked the stairways at the seventh floor and shut down the phones and elevators. They threatened to destroy the computers if the police were called in.

I saw the start of the latest sit-in early the next morning as I headed downtown. Students were milling around the main entrance. They appeared to me to be about equally divided between those sympathetic to the protestors who had taken over the university and those who were pissed off because their own classes had been cancelled. A secretary at the school who I knew came downtown to see if she could find out how long the protest might last and whether she'd be paid for her forced days off.

The most amazing display of protest and vandalism I witnessed came while standing at lunch hour in front of the building and watching students occupying the upper floors throwing armfuls of computer punch cards from the building. The cards fluttered down like giant confetti-snowflakes covering the streets and sidewalks.

By the time the riot squad entered the fray on February 11, the protestors had set a fire in the facilities. The Computer Center sustained $2 million in damages—the most costly destruction of property at any Canadian university to date.

Ninety-seven people were arrested and dragged out of the building in handcuffs. Sixty-nine of those arrested were students at Sir George. More than half were white.

Colin never ran a story on the riots. "It's too fast moving for us," he said each time something new developed. "The only thing our readers are interested in is what happened on Saturday night."

CHAPTER 31

I PLAYED THE guitar and wrote songs. I started a new novel and worked on a lengthier film treatment for *Mourning Flowers*, the low-budget crime film I had been working on since I had given up trying to rewrite my first novel. The treatment was about a man hiding out from his past who takes refuge in the countryside with two beautiful, sociopathic women. It was a tribute to a film I had seen years earlier in Los Angeles, *Les Félins*, with Alain Delon and Jane Fonda.

Love continued to elude me. I decided to try celibacy. That lasted about two weeks.

I drifted in and out of deep affection and lust—with Dee, who wanted to love me to death; with Cara, who preferred a poet I introduced her to; with the flower girl, who cruised the bars at happy hour, selling roses and vanished one day without leaving a forwarding address. Michelle, the actress who was living with her French boyfriend in an open relationship, suggested all three of us live together as husbands and wife. She said it was a common practice in Tibet. No, I said. I preferred my solitude.

I heard from old girlfriends from my California days. Anna had married a fellow Latin American Communist in Israel. She had returned to Mexico to have her first child and was still unhappy with life. Tess, who came from a wealthy Los Angeles family, had married well and had been having a torrid affair all through the marriage with a bank teller, who had just told her he was homosexual. Tess's husband had also shot her father in the face with birdshot on a hunting trip. Her father was healing nicely. Tess was thinking about leaving the US for Canada.

Who is the right one? Is there a right one? Is everyone the right one, I wondered.

My head spun. I knew what I wanted. I'd known for a long time. I wanted a woman who was mysterious, complicated, unpredictable, surprising, exciting, passionate beyond my own desires, and the most beautiful woman I had ever seen. With just as much fervor, I also wanted a woman who was down-to-earth, uncomplicated, trustworthy, thoroughly in love with me, beautiful to me but at the same time someone who wouldn't be relentlessly pursued by other men, and who was wise, calm, and nurturing. I wanted too much and was deserving of nothing.

✱ ✱ ✱

On February 13, 1969, the FLQ detonated their largest bomb to date since the start of their terrorist campaign, seriously injuring twenty-seven people and causing major damage to the Montreal Stock Exchange. The new bombing marked the beginning of a sixth wave of terror since the first wave of bombings in 1963. Organized by a new and more determined group of radicals, it would soon escalate into even greater violence and terror.

The Stock Exchange was just over a mile from my office in one direction and my apartment in another. As someone who had just invested in a mutual fund and a mining company, I took notice. I still held out hope that I could fit into Canada, but my failure to grasp French and my steady drift into English-language Montreal was a daily reminder that I was a minority in my new city.

✱ ✱ ✱

I first saw Sarah at Le Bistro moving through the crowd like a dolphin, touching this one lightly on the back, kissing that one, laughing. She seemed to know everyone and to be liked by everyone.

We caught each other's eye. We made a connection, stronger than words, wrapped in the mutual attraction of two strangers. I saw her again at the Pub and the Boiler Room. Sarah knew several people I knew—Alan, the bartender at the Boiler Room, Daniel, the artist who had introduced me to Margaux, and Ben, the manager of the Pub. I didn't need an introduction. She approached me the next time we crossed paths in the Boiler Room. She already knew my name, just as I had found out hers. We both knew right away we would sleep together.

Sarah lived in a rented room in the student ghetto. She was a tall, thin, dark-haired, dark-eyed very intense nineteen-year-old Jewish dancer who spoke six languages. Her native tongue was Hungarian. She had arrived in Canada with her parents as refugees from the Hungarian Revolt in the mid-1950s. She spent part of her youth in foster homes and institutions and left home in her early teens. She learned English and French in school and picked up several more languages on the streets and waterfront of Montreal. She used her language skills as a go-between and translator for sailors recently arrived by ship with hashish to sell to local small-time hashish dealers, who roamed the clubs downtown and in Old Montreal. When I met her, she was dealing small quantities of hashish to the downtown crowd to pick up extra money to give her the freedom to work on and off as a dancer in small theater and dance productions, which paid almost nothing.

One night about a week after the Stock Exchange bombing, I was sitting in my living room playing my guitar, working on a new song, and waiting for Sarah to show up as she usually did after her happy hour rounds, when my doorbell buzzed.

I assumed Sarah had forgotten her key. I hit the buzzer at the top of my landing, releasing the latch to the front door below.

My smile quickly faded as two hefty men in overcoats and fur hats filled the doorway.

"Joseph Glazner?" They looked and sounded like cops.

"Yes?"

"RCMP." They gave their names. "Can we come in? We'd like to talk to you."

The two Royal Canadian Mounted Policemen, the federal equivalent in Canada of the FBI, were halfway up the stairs already. Every cell in my body was on full alert.

"What's this about?"

"We'd like to ask you some questions."

The one in front was the friendlier of the two. He did all the talking at first, while the other one seemed to be scrutinizing everything—from me to the walls, floor, and ceiling.

Nothing will get past him, I thought.

"You live here alone?" the friendly one asked as I led them through the hall into the living room.

"Yes," I said, not really lying because Sarah still had her own place though she rarely slept there.

I was still living pretty lean. The only thing I had added to my meager furniture in my cavernous living room was a cheap portable stereo in the far corner on the floor. Several of my paintings, including some large nudes, stared out from the walls. One big canvas of an enormous pink nude hung near the kitchen entrance covering a gaping hole in the plaster.

"Nice paintings," the friendly officer said. "Yours?"

"Yes."

The quiet one finally broke his silence. He took out a notepad and pen, and asked me when I had arrived in Canada, when I had gotten my landed immigrant status, and the name and address of the company I worked for.

I gave him all the information. Oddly, he didn't write a thing down. I suspected he already knew the answers.

"Are you planning on staying in Canada?" the friendly one asked.

"Of course. Yes. What's this all about?" I asked again, politely but firmly, hoping my trembling knees wouldn't give me away.

The friendly one frowned. "We had an inquiry from the FBI in the US. They wanted to find out if you were still here. We stopped by to see if you were thinking about returning."

"I'm here to stay," I said. "Anything else?"

The two officers exchanged glances. "No. That's it. Thanks for your time."

On the way out, the friendly Mountie pointed at one of the nudes, and said, "I like that one."

And then they were gone.

I called my mother right after the door closed. She told me my FBI agent had visited their place in New Jersey the previous day. He had been by a couple of times since his first visit.

"I was going to tell you in my next letter," Mom told me. "I won't have to now."

So what were the Mounties doing at my place on St. Urbain Street? Did they really just show up in order to see if I was okay? Were they keeping an eye on me for the FBI? How closely was I being watched? Would they be coming back? If so, when? Their visit was a strong reminder that I was a fugitive.

Sarah was sure they were spying on *her*.

Something changed in the ether between us after that. Sarah became more wary of being at my place, fearful that the RCMP would return. I became more wary of having her there. I worried she would attract the RCMP or the local cops with her dope dealings.

We soon drifted apart, more out of inertia than design. The separation was more painful than I expected even though I knew we had to split up.

Zeke finally got fired at the end of February. He was never sure of the exact date. No one ever formally fired him because he hadn't been to the office in weeks.

The Suit came by my desk one afternoon to tell me, "If you see Zeke, tell him he's no longer employed here. I put through the paperwork. He can pick up his last paycheck at reception."

I saw Zeke over the weekend. He didn't want to talk about *Midnight*. Every ounce of his energy was focused on his new movie.

"We're getting close to signing. We should have everything in place within a month. I'm with the director and producer all day. It's a trip, Joseph, calling Europe in the morning, New York in the middle of the day, and Hollywood in the evening, talking to agents, actors, art directors, cameramen, makeup artists—finding out who's available and when. It's like putting together a Swiss watch with hundreds of parts that all have to work together."

The director had already made a few low-budget feature films. The producer had worked as a publicist at 20th Century Fox. Zeke said he was very well connected. Their movie had been given the green light. The final paperwork was just getting signed and once the first check arrived they would begin shooting.

Zeke's wife, Candice, was also enjoying a boost in her career. She had been cast as one of the four lead actors in a CBC comedy series that ran in the late afternoon. It was aimed at pre-teens and young teens with a goofy set of sketches and zany characters.

Zeke promised to introduce me to the director and the producer.

A few days before my twenty-fourth birthday while I was at home playing my guitar, I got a phone call from Johnny Vader.

"My father had a heart attack this afternoon. He's gone." Johnny sounded absolutely devastated. A neighbor had seen his father walking unsteadily down the street in the middle of the afternoon and thought he might be drunk. "When the medics found him, he was half in and half out of his truck, already dead." It seemed like a miserable and senseless death.

I hadn't thought of Johnny as a son until then. Husband and father, yes, but not a son. It hit me hard. I thought of my own father and how I hadn't really seen much of him in the past six years. When I had, he seemed so frail and miserable. I wondered if I would be as wrecked as Johnny was if I lost my father. Part of me said, no; part of me hoped I would be. The callous side of me continued to compete with my humane side. I still had no idea which would win. I knew I needed to stay hard and perhaps get tougher to survive. I wanted to distance myself from death. At the same time, I worried about losing my compassion for others.

I went to Johnny's house to sit *Shiva* with him, his wife, his young son, and his stepdaughter and stepson from his wife's first marriage. Johnny seemed so depressed, so knocked out by the loss that I wished I could do or say something to make him feel better. Of course, I could do nothing.

"I'll be off work until further notice. You and The Suit have to put out the paper by yourselves."

I was game. The Suit knew every aspect of the business. He could have put out the newspaper without me, but he treated me like a partner, and I got along well with him through the next few issues.

Jackie covers were still breaking circulation records. "Greek Police Reveal...PLOT TO KIDNAP JACKIE'S KIDS" did exceptionally well in February. Before Johnny went on bereavement leave, we had put together the "JACKIE'S SECRET LOVER" cover.

At the time, we were afraid of turning the newspaper into a Jackie magazine, though it was tempting. We continued to delude ourselves that we could actually saturate the market with too many Jackie stories.

We also still had a loyal readership base that craved sex, violence, and the unexplained. So we alternated with non-Jackie covers like "Exclusive Eyewitness Account: FLYING SAUCER KIDNAPS SHIP'S CAPTAIN."

With Johnny absent, The Suit tried another Sirhan cover. Sirhan was about to go on trial for the murder of Senator Kennedy. Sirhan requested the court issue an order to have him executed. The *Midnight* headline became: "SIRHAN ATTEMPTS SUICIDE."

It was a flop. We made up for the drop in circulation by creating another Jackie cover.

The Suit offered me Zeke's old job. I told him I'd think about it.

I really liked working with Johnny. He was one of the most decent, honest, and funniest co-workers I had ever had. But after six months with him, I felt I had learned most of the editing tricks. I wondered if a change might do me some good.

While I was trying to make up my mind, Johnny was suddenly summoned back from his bereavement leave earlier than he planned. We had a crisis onboard the mother ship.

CHAPTER 32

THE SUIT CALLED Johnny at home and insisted that he come in the next day. Johnny insisted he wasn't ready.

"You have to be here," The Suit kept pressuring him.

"What's this all about?"

"I can't tell you."

"Then, I can't come in."

The Suit finally blurted out, "Joe's selling the business."

Joe Azaria had just returned from an African safari and had decided to sell the tabloid business just as the *Sunday Express* was in its inaugural phase. Joe was keeping the *Sunday Express* and his newest acquisition, *The National Police Gazette*. The staff for the two papers would be moving to their own suite on a lower floor at the front of our building in April. Joe was leaving behind the rest of the newspapers and staff, including *Midnight*, Johnny, and me.

The new purchaser—if he could raise the money—was the company's chief financial guy. All the financial guy had to do was come up with the rumored million-dollar down payment. The rest, said to be between a million and five or six million, would be paid off in installments.

I felt tugged in all directions. The Suit wanted me to be his new assistant. Colin Gravenor told me he was looking for the right story to give me a try. Johnny would be happy if I stayed. By then, he referred to me as his associate editor. On the other hand, he knew I was already becoming restless.

Johnny, The Suit, and I did another Jackie cover with double headlines: "French Magazine Says: JACKIE IS HIDING THE TRUTH ABOUT JFK'S DEATH," and "New Orleans Exclusive, Garrison's Office Says: We'll Subpoena Jackie to Testify At Clay Shaw Trial."

Just when I was starting to get Jackie fatigue myself, a rare directive came down from Joe Azaria to go with another Jackie cover. Johnny said it was intended to keep the circulation as high as possible before the sale of the tabloids closed.

Coming so soon after the last Jackie cover, the usual Monday morning cover session kept dragging on and on with no one coming up with a headline we could agree on.

Finally, with my stomach growling, I joked, "Why not 'Jackie Is Frigid'?"

I waited for the laugh, but instead, Johnny shouted, "That's it, that's it."

He couldn't congratulate me enough.

When the stringer came in a few hours later to talk over the story, he asked, "Why is Jackie frigid, Joseph?"

"Because we need a cover story. Why else?"

Gallows humor. We concluded our meeting with peace signs, and the writer went on his way. I sat back, stared at the St. Lawrence River ambling by in the distance below my window, and told myself, "I need a change."

I finally took The Suit's offer.

Right after I became the new associate photo editor, Colin asked me if I had time to do a story for him.

CHAPTER 33

THE REASON THAT the FBI went to my parents' house in New Jersey and the RCMP came to visit me in Montreal shortly afterward in February was that my federal indictment had finally been issued. Amazingly, it had taken the government a year to indict me after I had failed to report for my induction.

I was now officially on the FBI's wanted list.

I cared that I might be ruining my future, but I had no reason to back down.

Vietnam may have been on the other side of the world, but it remained my war.

I wanted it to stop.

All winter, the killing continued in spite of the peace talks in Paris.

The US, South Vietnam, Viet Cong, and North Vietnam negotiators must all be assholes, I thought. They were all dragging their heels. None of the suits gave a shit about the wounded and dying soldiers and civilians.

Nixon's appointee, Henry Cabot Lodge replaced Johnson's appointee, Averell Harriman, for chief US negotiator. Lodge had been Nixon's Vice Presidential running mate in his failed Presidential bid in 1960.

While the diplomats haggled, the Viet Cong launched attacks on more than a hundred targets across Saigon and the rest of South Vietnam on February 23. Thirty-six Marines were killed at their base camp near the Demilitarized Zone (DMZ) during attacks by the North Vietnam Army on

February 25. On March 4, President Nixon threatened to resume bombing North Vietnam in retaliation for the attacks in South Vietnam. US troops resumed offensive action in the DMZ for the first time in 1969.

It made my stomach crawl knowing US troop levels in Vietnam were continuing to rise. [23]

Students and activists across North America were coming out in growing numbers to protest the war.

In Montreal, the Quebec separatist movement was growing in strength as well.

★ ★ ★

McGill University, the largely English-language university in the heart of the downtown, had become a major symbol of the English establishment's dominance over the ordinary French-speaking citizen. Even though many of the French elite and intellectuals like Gilles Carle had gone to McGill, and an equally revered, mainly French-language university—University of Montreal—operated on the other side of the mountain, many of the Quebec separatists eyed the English-language McGill as a key symbol in their fight to end the domination of the English speakers in Quebec.

As spring approached, the leaders of the Quebec separatist movement began organizing a mass demonstration to demand that McGill turn itself into a French-language institution.

I was assigned to cover the event for the *Sunday Express.*

The public was urged to gather on Friday night, March 28 in Carré St. Louis, the little square off St. Denis Street, a half-dozen blocks due east of my apartment.

It took me five minutes to walk there. I had heard the RCMP and provincial and city police would be out in full force.

My press pass was a hastily typed letter on *Sunday Express* letterhead with Colin's signature on the bottom. It said I was a reporter for the paper.

The crowd was as large as I expected but where were the police, I wondered as I made my way through the square in the near freezing weather. I saw no one in uniform in the crowd of thousands of trade unionists, separatists, and students milling around the square.

Were the police undercover? Were there any police present?

A mixed mood of anger, nervousness, and party-like jubilation hung over the crowd. The voices of the demonstrators milling around the square were much louder, the laughter more forced than the peacenik gatherings and love-ins I had attended in Los Angeles in years past.

More like a sporting event, I thought, making a mental note to write something about that. The participants were psyching each other up, creating an "us-and-them" mentality. They were getting ready to do battle. The English speakers were the enemy. The English language was a poison that choked off something good and native in their breasts.

How had it come to this, I kept wondering. I wanted to believe that people who spoke different languages and came from different nations could live peacefully side-by-side.

As I moved through the crowd, trying to figure out what to write, I ran into several Québécois acquaintances in different spots in the small park. None were good friends, but all had been friendly in the past. Not this night.

They had mob eyes, eyes out for blood, eyes that looked at me with hostility even when I greeted them in my few words of French.

"*Maudit anglais!*" I heard one of them tell his friend as he turned away from me.

I'm a reporter, I wanted to explain. A neutral. But I would have had to explain in English. Not a good idea.

I remained in the square while the leaders of the march delivered their fiery speeches, raising the pulse of the crowd to a blood boiling, cheering single voice of a lynch mob or a crowd at a boisterous football game. Of course, I couldn't understand more than a word here and there—and definitely not enough to put together a coherent sentence about what this group of students and unionists thought the issues really were.

As the crowd poured out of the square, marched down St. Denis Street to Sherbrooke Street, and turned west toward the McGill Gates, I worried about how I was ever going to write a story with so little understanding of what was taking place.

More and more people joined the swelling parade from the side streets.

The faces at the front of the procession had the jut-chinned, cold-eyed stares of those dreaming of being the next Che Guevara, Fidel Castro,

Mao, or Lenin. I imagined myself as Charlie Chaplin or Harpo Marx, trying to silently convey what I was seeing and feeling.

I stayed with the slow-moving crowd for a few minutes before hurrying ahead toward the campus, hoping to get a good position at the gates to witness the moment of arrival of the half-festive, half-angry army when they finally reached McGill. I was hoping to see something unique.

I presented my press letter to a cop in front of the gates and watched as it was passed around by several uniformed police and Mounties until someone gave the nod to let me pass through the gates and join the small army of city riot police, provincial police, RCMP officers, security guards, and reporters waiting for the marchers.

That evening back at my place I tapped out the following:

Friday, 28 March 1969

Ten thousand Montrealers participated Friday night in what appears to be a new citywide spectator sport—demonstration watching.

The spectators were on hand to watch Canada's answer to the bullfight.

An estimated 1,200 hardcore demonstrators paraded down Sherbrooke Street to the McGill campus accompanied by thousands of roaring, cheering fans who pushed their way down Sherbrooke hoping for a view of their favorite toreadors. Thousands crowded along the sidewalks, onto doorsteps, and windowsills of the buildings facing the McGill Gates between University and Stanley Streets. By the time the demonstrators arrived at nine o'clock, the crowd had swelled to an SRO audience, turning the area into what looked like a huge arena. The political and intellectual motif of the demonstration vanished after a few slogans were chanted and was replaced with a frivolous, carnival atmosphere. The audience waited for the show to begin.

Then, for an uneventful hour and a half, the toreadors faced off with the bulls, mobilized *en masse* behind the gates of the campus on the north side of Sherbrooke. Several self-styled matadors tried to goad the police into charging by burning placards, shouting obscenities, and lighting firecrackers, but nothing happened. There were several moments when it actually looked as though the frustrated matadors might charge the bulls, but again nothing happened. Only a few wooden sticks used to hold up placards and a half-dozen Roman candles ever managed to penetrate the police cordon.

Much to the disappointment of the spectators—husbands and wives, young men out with their dates, thrill seekers, students, hippies, motorcycle gangs, concerned businessmen, and several old ladies out walking their dogs—the matadors never succeeded in provoking the bulls into a charge.

In fact, when the police decided the demonstration should end, the audience dispersed peacefully and without major incident. A handful of spectators frustrated that the show had been called off before the anticipated and traditional bloodletting and kill of either the matador or the bull, stayed behind, causing minor damage to the arena.

In the end, the event was conceded to the bull—the match was a bore. But that's Canadian bull fighting for you.

✲ ✲ ✲

The next morning I delivered my copy to Colin Gravenor's house and waited with great trepidation in a chair beside him at his breakfast table while he read my story.

"Nicely done. Well written. You're a good writer, Joseph," he finally said, looking up from the last page.

I'm in, I thought. I wanted to jump up and shout for joy.

"But we can't use it. Sorry." He returned the pages to me.

I stared at the sheets of paper for a second, trying to grasp what I had just heard. Finally, I mumbled, "Why not? You said it was good."

"It is. It's just not news anymore. Nothing really happened. You said so yourself. If we were a Saturday paper, then maybe we could print it in this morning's edition. By tomorrow morning, no one'll care what happened on Friday, because nothing happened."

That was it. Colin was sorry. "I'll give you another assignment as soon as one comes up, but there's nothing on the horizon," he told me.

I wondered if he was just letting me down gently.

"If you have any ideas, you can always bring them to me. You're a good writer," he repeated.

In spite of what Colin said, I felt defeated and broken. I took solace in the fact that I still had my new job with The Suit but that was already getting to me.

CHAPTER 34

I WAS BEGINNING to understand what compelled me to want to be a writer.

It was something I thought I could do to earn a living.

I also felt safe when I wrote. It was almost a form of hypnotism as I put myself deep in a cocoon of my own thoughts where the world slowed down enough so I could make more sense of it. I liked the process of stopping or at least slowing down the constant dialogue in my head, grabbing just the right thoughts, and trying to write them down or typing them before they vanished. Life made more sense because I could write.

I dreamed of writing something wonderful, something that would explode in other people's heads like the best of the books had done in mine.

I was uncertain how I would ever achieve that. I found myself constantly torn between staying home and writing—a new song, a few pages of a novel, an idea for a movie, or a letter home or to one of my friends; painting (which I treated as a form of storytelling); writing in my journals about how I was feeling and thinking—or going out, hanging around the bars, looking for characters, listening to stories, falling in love, and trying to find a life that would be exciting enough to write about.

Part of me said that I would only write something good when I had truly fallen in love. Part of me said that I would never attract a beautiful, intelligent woman who would want to be with me forever unless I was a more successful writer.

I wasn't even sure what I should be writing, but I was sure that I had to write even if it meant letting Sisyphus take up permanent residence in my brain.

* * *

One of *Midnight's* stringers, who supplied medical photos of mutilated corpses and deformities in the old days, sent in a horrifying photo of a deformed infant.

Johnny instantly knew what the cover that week should be.

The headline screamed: "COLA DID THIS TO MY BABY." The story was cleverly crafted to appear to be about the most popular brands of cola but written in just such a way to avoid a lawsuit.

Mixed in with the utterly depraved publication of the photo was a moral lesson that I could approve of. The brown, sugar-and-caffeine-laced sodas that were rotting our teeth were also doing untold damage to our organs and genes, or so I had heard in the underground press.

Maybe the scare story would keep a few people from guzzling too much soda.

I proposed putting a napalmed baby on the cover of *Midnight* with the headline, "War Did This to My Baby."

Johnny thought I was joking. I was already becoming restless in my new job after only a couple of weeks.

I knew it was only a matter of time before I followed Zeke out the door. I began to save as much as I could from each paycheck.

CHAPTER 35

I ASSUMED THAT life at The Globe Newspaper Group would be business as usual once the sale of *Midnight* and the other tabloids went through. The possibility of massive changes never occurred to me. The financial guy struck me as a hands-off manager, who would inevitably leave everything on the editorial side as is.

I assumed The Suit was happy to be staying. Ditto Johnny. I assumed they both had close ties with the financial guy after all the years they had been working together. So I believed I was as secure as I could be. I assumed Joe and the financial guy were on friendly terms and would remain so. As a result, I thought nothing of going for lunch with The Suit to meet Joe, Colin, and some of the others from the *Sunday Express* on the day Joe and the financial guy finalized the deal.

Joe Azaria had been holding court at lunchtime in the Sir Winston Churchill Pub on Crescent Street for many months.

The Sir Winston Churchill Pub and its sister club, the Boiler Room, had already become two of the most popular centers of downtown nightlife in Montreal by the spring of 1969. They were two of a half-dozen clubs where I could go to any time and be recognized by the owners, staff, and scores of the regulars.

The Pub had opened just over a month after I first arrived at Emile's place. The bar and restaurant were located a half a block down the hill on the other side of Crescent Street in the basement of an old stone row house. The owner was one of downtown Montreal's most celebrated characters, Johnny Vago. The Hungarian-born Vago, by then in his mid-forties, had led a colorful life, studying architecture in Western Europe and Montreal after the Second World War, and introducing espresso and the outdoor café to Montreal. Vago built some of the most popular restaurants and nightspots in the city in the 1950s before getting bored and heading to Cuba where he continued doing business before and after the Revolution. A friend and confidante of Che Guevara and Fidel Castro, Vago had even represented the post-revolution Cuba on a trade mission to Europe for Castro.

After returning to Montreal in the mid-sixties, Vago opened new nightclubs in the downtown, including the Don Juan, the Pub, and most recently, the Boiler Room.

Joe Azaria, a contemporary of Vago's and someone who was equally well known around the Montreal bar scene, was a rumored investor in the Pub. When Joe wanted to cash out, Vago allegedly paid him back with food and drink for a year. Joe regularly ate and drank lunch there.

Colin Gravenor, a couple of his pretty editorial assistants from the *Sunday Express*, The Suit, and I waited for Joe to arrive from his meeting with the financial guy, Johnny Vader, and another old timer. Joe had gone to that meeting to receive the check from the financial guy and sign the final papers for the sale of the tabloids. Johnny was at the meeting because he was considered a key player, and because, when Joe had originally incorporated, he had given Johnny a few shares to conform to laws requiring officers of the company to hold an interest.

Our outing at the Pub was running later than I had anticipated. By one-thirty, we'd been there an hour and a half, and Joe still hadn't shown up. We had eaten lunch but were still working our way through gallons of alcoholic beverages when I started thinking about heading back. When I told The Suit, he said, "What's your hurry? Stay." The Suit was my boss. I stayed.

Finally, closer to two o'clock, Joe arrived and greeted us warmly. He ordered another round of drinks and joined the conversation, which was mainly focused on the coming edition of the *Sunday Express*.

All very interesting, I told myself, but I finally decided to return to the office and mop up the remainder of the tasks I had for the afternoon. The Suit stayed at the Pub.

Everyone except Johnny was at their desks when I showed up about two-thirty. Johnny had left early that day to try to sell his father's truck.

"The new big boss wants to see you," one of the editors said as soon as I reached my desk.

"Oh?"

"He came by a half hour ago looking for The Suit, too."

"The Suit's still at the Pub. I'll go tell the boss." I headed down the hall to the financial guy's office, curious but not particularly concerned.

"You want to see me?" I asked standing in his open doorway.

"Yes. Come in. Sit down." He didn't get up or smile.

"I understand you're looking for The Suit," I said.

"Do you know where he is?"

"Probably still at the Pub. He was supposed to have lunch with Joe, but Joe arrived late."

He didn't respond but instead handed me a check. "This is for you."

I looked at the numbers. It was for just over two hundred dollars. My first thought: This is a bonus, something to do with the sale of the company.

"That's your last two weeks' pay and a week's vacation with deductions taken out."

I looked down at the check again, my mind in a complete whirl. The amount was just what I would expect after taxes for three weeks' pay.

"I don't understand," I said, still clinging to the idea that maybe this had something to do with the end of the old accounting regime and the beginning of the new one.

"We're closing down your department." He explained that one of the other junior executives was taking over the work of The Suit and me.

"Maybe I can work for one of the other papers," I said lamely.

"No."

I thought I caught a little smile forming at the corners of his mouth.

"So I'm being fired?"

He folded his hands on the desk in front of him and said nothing.

As I headed out the door, he added, "I didn't have to give you the vacation pay."

Wow, I thought as I headed back to my desk to pick up my personal possessions. I've just been fired.

Far out.

It was the first time I had ever been fired. I hadn't seen it coming. I had no idea what to do. It seemed surreal.

CHAPTER 36

I EARNED THE bragging rights for being the first person fired under the new ownership.

The Suit claimed he resigned. The Suit never returned to the office that afternoon. Johnny told me on the phone later that he had been told by the new management that anyone having contact with The Suit or me would be fired.

★ ★ ★

At the time I was fired—the last week of April 1969—I had officially been a landed immigrant for exactly a year. I had already had three jobs, two of which had collapsed due to mismanagement or lack of funds. The third ended because I had been so completely naïve about office politics that I never guessed how much animosity existed between the financial guy and The Suit.

It didn't matter how hard I worked or what was promised to me. The work environment was completely and utterly unpredictable and ruthless. It was really no one's fault. It was just the way of the world. Like it or not, I was on the street again.

I was on shaky ground. Writing jobs in English were scarce, and any job that I saw in the newspapers in the social welfare field always wanted bilingual applicants only.

Equally troubling, my investment in my IOS mutual funds was already down thirty percent. My nickel and bismuth mine in the Northwest Territories had done even worse, sinking so low that the selling commission would eat up the remaining value.

I called my broker and asked him what I should do. He said to hold on. That was what he was doing. [24]

I looked for work everywhere, even in the garment factories along St. Lawrence. No one seemed to be hiring.

The Suit immediately started a new French-language tabloid and was camping out at the *Sunday Express* offices a couple of floors below the Globe while he pulled his new venture together.

Colin Gravenor had plenty of seasoned journalists stringing for him, but he told me, "I'm still looking for the right story for you." I pitched him a few ideas but none that excited him.

Bob Russel and I had lunch in Old Montreal. Bob had lots of ideas for Orbafilm but no money. He was operating the shop by himself again and depressed. "I'll call you if anything turns up." We would reconnect, and I would play a role in the resurrection of his think tank but that would be more than a year in the future.

In my immediate future, I had great hope in Zeke's producer. He was very interested in *Mourning Flowers*, the most developed of my film treatments. I had just completed a new version of my story.

"I'll get you some development money as soon as our financing comes through," he said.

★ ★ ★

I started hanging around the local underground newspaper, *Logos*. Their office was on Clark Street a few blocks from me. The paper had been in existence about a year and had been busted numerous times, including several instances where street vendors had been pinched selling papers without a license, which the city had refused to give them.

The newspaper had gone through some rough patches in the past few months and was in a tug-of-war between a new, young, hip rich kid who claimed to be an expert in astrology and whose money seemed to come from selling LSD, and a small clique of leftist radicals and political activists, a few of whom were draft resisters and deserters, and all of whom were long on rhetoric but short on business sense and editorial experience.

The rich kid wanted me to take over as editor. Since he had no money to pay me, I declined but kept an eye on the place in case it might get back on its feet.

Peter Lebensold was in the midst of founding a new magazine called *the five cent review...a monthly review of the arts in Canada.* He asked me to be one of his book reviewers. No pay at the moment, of course, but I was in good company since other book reviewers included such future famous Canadian writers as Doug Fetherling, Nick Auf der Maur, and former musician Zal Yanovsky, late of the *Loving Spoonful* and then living in Montreal and developing a Court TV television series. I was friends with both Nick and Zal through the common drinking spots we frequented.

The nice thing about my assignment for the inaugural issue of the magazine was that Peter assigned me to read a Bernard Malamud book, an author I was familiar with. Peter published my review just as I wrote it.

Peter Lebensold was also friends with National Film Board director Robin Spry. Spry was putting together his first feature film, a docudrama called *Prologue,* about a Montreal draft resister and a Montreal underground newspaper editor who take different paths—one character taking to the streets and participating in the riots that accompanied the 1968 Democratic Convention in Chicago, and the other retreating with his girlfriend to a commune. Spry wanted a guitar-playing draft resister and asked Peter if he knew anyone who might fit. Peter suggested me. So guitar in hand, I trekked out to the sprawling factory-like headquarters of the NFB and had a long meeting with Spry who noticeably winced when I played him one of my songs.

I didn't get a call back.

✶ ✶ ✶

I also secretly kept in touch with Johnny Vader by phone at his home. "I'm sorry you got fired. I knew the new boss was going to fire The Suit but not you or I would have warned you. If you weren't blackballed I'd have plenty of work for you," he told me.

That got me thinking, and soon, I came up with a shadowy plan. I talked to a writer friend of mine who was always looking for work. When the writer agreed to be my go-between for a small percentage, I called Johnny again. "Would it work if I got a writer friend of mine to pick up assignments and bring them back to you? His name would be on all the assignments and checks."

"Can you trust him?" he asked.

"A hundred percent," I told him, knowing Johnny's job was on the line.

Johnny couldn't risk giving me too many stories at a time, but he did feed me enough work that I had a trickle of income each month.

On Monday, May 26, nearly a month after I'd been fired, I dropped by Jean-Claude Pilon's studio on St. Catherine Street hoping to pick up some small tidbit of work.

"I have something you might be interested in," he told me. "I have a new contract from the Man and His World Exhibition to provide a short film for the Strange, Strange World exhibit. Are you familiar with it?"

"Yes. I took my parents to see it last summer." Strange, Strange World (also called the Strange, Strange World Pavilion) was housed in the old Canadian Pavilion at the old Expo '67 site. The exhibit was part science, part unexplained phenomena.

Strange, Strange World had been so successful the previous year that the exhibit executives wanted to expand it. Jean-Claude had been hired to create a film that could be looped and shown continuously as one of the centerpieces of the improved exhibit. Jean-Claude envisioned the film as a showcase of all of the available film footage in the world on the most popular, unexplained phenomena caught on film to date.

To help locate and bring the footage to Montreal, Jean-Claude began collaborating with one of the foremost investigators in the field of unusual phenomena, British-American author, scientist, and television personality, Ivan T. Sanderson, founder and head of the Society for the Investigation of the Unexplained in New Jersey. Sanderson was already a consultant to Michael Lambert, the designer and brains behind the original concept for the Strange, Strange World exhibit.

"Your job is to work with Sanderson in any capacity he needs," Jean-Claude explained. Sanderson's mandate was to locate all the available film footage of space aliens, Unidentified Flying Objects, Loch Ness Monsters, and various half-human, half-ape-like creatures allegedly sighted in different regions of the world in ancient and modern times and known by such names as the Sasquatch Monster, the Abominable Snowman, Big Foot, and Yeti.

"Meet him at his suite on the ninth floor of the Queen Elizabeth Hotel at nine in the morning," Jean-Claude told me that day.

This should be fun, I thought, especially since Jean-Claude was always a generous contractor. He was paying me more than I had made in a week at *Midnight*.

I also felt a sense of trepidation after being fired. I wanted to do a good job. I slept badly that night, worried once again about failure.

★ ★ ★

On Tuesday morning, May 27, as I was just heading out my door to meet Sanderson and start my new gig, the phone rang.

Afraid to be late, I almost didn't answer it. I changed my mind at the last minute and grabbed the phone, thinking maybe it had something to do with my meeting.

I recognized the gruff voice on the other end of the line right away. It was Colin Gravenor from the *Sunday Express*.

"I have an assignment for you if you want it," he said.

This was the phone call I had been hoping to get. It showed up at exactly the wrong time. I almost said, no. My week was already booked, but I still had to ask, "What's the story?"

"John Lennon's just arrived in town. He and his new wife are holding a Bed-In for Peace like the one they did in Amsterdam. I'd like you to do a story on Lennon and his thoughts on draft dodgers and their contribution to peace. They're holding a press conference at the Queen Elizabeth Hotel at noon for the Montreal press. Can you do it?"

Amazing, I thought. The Queen Elizabeth Hotel was the same hotel where I was meeting Ivan T. Sanderson. The gods were conspiring to make me say yes. Surely I could go to my first meeting and then pop over to the press conference at noon. Sanderson had to eat lunch, didn't he?

Not surprisingly, given my nervous state, I still almost said no. I was scared by the prospect of writing under pressure, especially since I had no idea how much work I'd have to do for Sanderson and our flying saucer film. I also didn't want to fail Colin in what I hoped might be my first paying assignment for the *Sunday Express*.

"Come to the office, and we'll go to the conference together," he said.

"I can't," I blurted out, hoping against hope that I wasn't killing my chances. "I've got another meeting in the morning."

"Then you can meet me there," he insisted. I sensed he'd already made up his mind that he wanted me to do this article. The moment to say no had passed.

"Where should I meet you?"

"Go to room 1742. Ask for Derek Taylor. He's the contact person for the conference. I'll see you there at noon."

☆ ☆ ☆

I was in a daze as I headed outside and down the hill toward the hotel.

Derek Taylor, Derek Taylor, Derek Taylor, I kept saying over and over.

I recognized the name instantly. More than recognized it. It gave me goose bumps. Derek Taylor was the Beatles' first press agent and the late Brian Epstein's personal assistant. He had also been the Los Angeles public relations guru for the Beach Boys, Mamas and Papas, Byrds, Paul Revere and the Raiders, and other rock royalty when I lived there. He was a co-founder and organizer of the Monterey International Pop Festival. He was Mike Vosse's friend, and Mike Vosse's boss at the pop festival.

Mike Vosse was a close friend of mine from university days in Los Angeles. He had introduced me to Derek Taylor.

Derek Taylor was the same Derek Taylor who I had met and spent an afternoon with at his house in October 1967. He was on an acid trip. I was about to take off for Canada.

"I know you," Derek had said, holding his hand palm out in greeting when Mike introduced us at his front door. He had greeted me like an old friend arriving from another planet.

Wondering if he'd remember me, I was excited and a bit crazed as I got closer to the hotel.

Maybe I could pull together a group of war resisters to meet John Lennon.

Maybe this is my chance to show I'm not a complete fuck-up.

I quickened my pace. My mind was whirling.

CHAPTER 37

I TRIED TO recall what I had heard and read about John Lennon in the past few months.

John and Yoko had married in March. They held their honeymoon in Amsterdam as a publicity vehicle. They called it a Bed-In, a takeoff on Be-In, Love-In, and Sit-In. The Bed-In was supposed to promote world peace and demonstrate a novel, non-violent method to protest against the Vietnam War—stay in bed, be creative, make love. They were also publicly displaying their love and commitment to live, love, and work together.

John admitted during their Amsterdam Bed-In that Apple was in bad financial shape. The peace campaign was a genuine attempt to do something positive, he said, but he also was not at all adverse to the media mentioning new Beatles or Lennon recordings. The Amsterdam event had been widely covered in Europe but received only scant coverage in the US and Canada.

As silly as it was, I liked the idea of a peaceful protest against the war by the most famous musician on the planet. The war needed protesting. It kept escalating in spite of Nixon's secret plan. Nearly a half-million American military personnel were in Vietnam. More that 33,000 Americans and hundreds of thousands of North and South Vietnamese soldiers and civilians had already been killed. [25]

It was good to see someone as powerful and media savvy as John Lennon lending his voice to the growing anti-war movement. The Amsterdam Bed-In was, in my mind, the first time that a Beatle had really shouted out against the Vietnam War. Yoko, I'd heard, had steered John toward the peace and anti-war movement as a cause they should focus on together.

They had been through a lot together in the past few months.

John and Yoko's second album, *Unfinished Music No. 2, Life with the Lions*, had been released earlier in the month. The cover featured a photo of Yoko in a London hospital the previous November after she had suffered her miscarriage of the child she conceived with John. John, clean-shaven and wearing wire rim glasses, lay on the floor beside the hospital bed, looking utterly forlorn. The back cover was of John and Yoko leaving a London police station after their hashish-cannabis bust in October 1968, which was said to have triggered the miscarriage.

Most recently, the US Embassy in London had used John's drug conviction to deny Lennon a visa to visit the US.

Determined to fight back, Lennon had been trying to get into the US for the past few days to promote his new album and hold a second Bed-In with Yoko. They had already flown to Freeport, Bahamas and tried to clear entry into the US from there. When John was again refused clearance to enter the US, he and Yoko flew to Toronto where they seemed to have caused only a minor stir on the media radar. Finally, they flew to Montreal, where a few hundred fans greeted them at the airport when they arrived at midnight.

What I didn't know at the time was that within a few days the Beatles would be releasing their latest single—"The Ballad of John and Yoko," a song written by John with input from Paul McCartney. It was about John's relationship with Yoko, recorded by John and Paul in the middle of April. The scheduled release date was on May 30, 1969. [26]

The Bed-In was silently geared to promote "The Ballad of John and Yoko." It was an unabashed record-promoting publicity stunt. A gimmick, as they themselves called it. It was no different than the cross-branding and celebrity branding used by corporate America, except it would likely be a lot more fun.

When I had heard on the radio that morning that John and Yoko were coming to town, I hadn't really thought about it because it had nothing to do with me.

Now, it suddenly was about me—at least, in the sense that I had a chance to interview someone famous and try to get a story out of it.

★ ★ ★

I saw a dozen media people and early-bird fans milling around the lobby of the hotel. Hotel staff and uniformed security guards kept them away from the elevators.

I headed straight for the elevators as if I belonged.

A liveried hotel staffer made straight for me.

"I'm here to see Ivan Sanderson," I told him when he blocked my way.

He flagged his manager. I gave them Sanderson's room number. "I have an appointment."

The manager steered me to the front desk and phoned Sanderson, and I was soon on my way to the ninth floor on an empty elevator.

Ivan T. Sanderson, a tall, fit, well-dressed, handsome older man with a neatly trimmed goatee, greeted me at the door with a warm smile and friendly eyes. "So nice to meet you," he said in a strong, comforting voice with a British accent. "Can you give me a few minutes? I'm just finishing some work on another project."

He had ordered coffee, toast, and orange juice for us, and he left me in one corner with the food while he went to the desk in the other corner of the room and began typing away on a strange looking typewriter.

I poured myself a cup of coffee and watched him type, fascinated by the metal brace holding a roll of paper over his typewriter. The paper fed continuously into the typewriter so he didn't have to stop at the end of the page and insert another sheet.

"Done," he finally said, looking up after several more minutes of typing.

"Where did you get the typewriter?" I asked.

"It's a regular typewriter," he said. "I invented the continuous feed attachment. Pretty handy when I'm writing a book."

The guy's a genius, I thought.

Over breakfast, he told me about the research institute he had founded to study the unexplained. He lived in an ancient house in rural New Jersey near the Delaware River, close to where I had spent many summers at various YMCA and Boy Scout camps. He was fifty-eight, the same age as my father. He had been in the British Navy during the Second World War and was a hundred percent against Vietnam.

"I like your generation. Perhaps you'll find a way for us to get along better with everyone. We have to get rid of our prejudices." His wife, he told me, was an African princess from Madagascar. He produced a photo from his wallet of a beautiful black woman of indeterminate age and handed it to me. "She's a medical entomologist specializing in malaria. I met her in Paris before the war."

"She's very pretty."

He smiled. "Did you know that John Lennon and his new Japanese wife are in the hotel?"

My lucky day, I thought. He's following the news.

"I wanted to talk to you about that," I said. I told him about my John Lennon assignment. He seemed very interested. He kept asking me questions. I told him of my connection to Derek Taylor and how I was supposed to ask for him. I explained that I didn't have to go to the press conference until noon. "We could work all morning and then I could come back right afterward. You won't have to worry."

He smiled and thought for a moment. "This sounds like a very good opportunity for you. If I were you, I would head up there right now and see if your friend, Derek, has time to see you. If you wait until noon, the entire press corps will be there, and Derek might be too busy to talk."

"He may not remember me."

"If he doesn't, come back down, and we'll get started. Otherwise, stay there as long as you like. I have plenty of work I can do on my own. Call me this afternoon after the press conference or drop by. We'll talk. The fellow who's directing our film is meeting me here after lunch."

My heart was racing. "You're okay with me leaving right now?"

"Don't worry. I'm as curious as you about what's going on upstairs. I'm counting on you to come back and give me a full report." He smiled. "I am a Beatles fan, you know."

Funny, personable, charming, extremely intelligent—those were just some of the words I thought to describe my new boss. It wasn't lost on me that we hadn't talked at all about flying saucers, Abominable Snowmen, or Loch Ness Monsters.

Ivan was going to be great to work for, I told myself as I headed toward the seventeenth floor via the stairs, figuring I'd have less chance of running into hotel security than on the elevator.

✷ ✷ ✷

I was feeling pumped up from the climb as I anticipated crashing the event ahead of time. I was also undeniably nervous. I tried to figure out what I would say when I got to the suite. Would I even get to see Derek Taylor? Would he have time for me? Would he remember a twenty-two-year-old who spent an afternoon at his house in the Hollywood Hills while he was so high on acid, he kept telling me he knew me and could see into my soul?

I imagined an entourage of dozens of handlers surrounding John Lennon, a gauntlet of guards and henchmen who would likely tell me to get lost and come back at the appointed time.

I poked my head out the door of the stairwell into the hallway on the seventeenth floor. A housekeeper was gathering towels from a cart, and a security guard stood near the elevators with his back to me.

Head high, walking like I was on a mission, I headed in the opposite direction, making a beeline for Room 1742.

Before I had gone more than a half-dozen steps, the guard spotted me and immediately headed in my direction.

"Hey, you, what are you doing here?" he called.

I acted like I belonged. I kept going.

He hurriedly caught up to me and blocked my way. "What are you doing here?" he repeated.

"I have an appointment with Derek Taylor. He's expecting me," I said firmly.

His eyebrows went up. I knew instantly I had said the magic words—Derek Taylor.

"Okay." He stepped aside and let me pass.

I continued on my way alone toward the hotel room, trying to think what to say to the real gatekeepers inside.

I could still smell my own fear as I stood in front of 1742 seconds before finally getting my nerve up to knock.

CHAPTER 38

SECONDS AFTER I knocked, the door swung open, and I was standing face-to-face with Derek Taylor.

I thought I would have to go through layers of people before even seeing him. He was the last person I expected to see first.

My mind froze. "Uh, I'm...."

Derek raised his hand palm out to stop me. "I know who you are. You're Mike Vosse's friend, Joseph. The writer who was on his way to Canada. I see you made it." He grinned. He wasn't chasing me away. The open palm, the universal sign of peace, and a friendly smile were exactly how he greeted me high in the Hollywood Hills a year and a half ago, I thought.

"You remember." I was simultaneously delighted and dumbfounded that he recognized me.

"Of course, glad to see you. Come in, come in."

After a quick glance down the empty hallway, he waved me inside and shut the door behind us.

From beyond the doorway, deep in the darkened room I heard someone shout, "Don't let the press in yet, Derek. We're not ready."

That's John Lennon's voice, I thought as we moved into the room.

"It's all right, John," Derek said matter-of-factly, walking a half-step ahead of me. "He's one of us."

One of us. Wow, I thought as John Lennon looked up from the phone and at me for the first time.

John Lennon, bearded, wearing wire rim glasses and white pajamas, was sitting on the edge of the king-sized bed, talking on the phone. He held the receiver in one hand and a felt-tip black marker in the other. On the bed beside him was a white poster board with "HA" written on it in big bubble letters. He gave me a friendly nod and a smile, said a few more words into the phone, and hung up.

Derek introduced us. "Joseph's a friend from Los Angeles. He can help you, John." Then to me: "I have to look after a few things. We'll catch up later." He disappeared through the side door into the adjoining room.

"Can you draw?" John asked me, relaxed now and very warm like we had been friends since the beginning of time.

"Yes," I told him as he carried the poster he'd been working on to the floor at the foot of the bed to get a firmer writing surface to work on. I moved the handful of felt-tip markers and blank poster boards from the bedspread to the floor beside him.

He added "IR" in bubble letters to the "HA" to produce the word "HAIR" on the board.

"You can blacken in the letters," he told me, handing me the poster. "That should speed things up."

In addition to John and me, two other people were milling about the room, Nick Knowland, a cameraman, and Mike Lax, a sound man, both of whom had come from the UK with John, Yoko, and Derek. Nick and Mike were in a world by themselves setting up their equipment. They had no time to chat. [27]

At first, John and I worked in our own little world without speaking; he writing words like "Hair," "Peace," and "Bagism," in big bubble letters on the poster boards and me filling in the bubbles with a black felt-tip marker. Bagism was one of John and Yoko's latest ideas. The term had been introduced in their Vienna press conference in March. Yoko and John had covered themselves in a bag and delivered their message through the cloth to reporters, explaining that the bag was meant as a humorous way to separate their message of peace from their visual celebrity—blocking out the listeners' prejudices toward race, color, age, gender, the length of a person's hair, and other personal attributes that could get in the way of the message. The Lennons had been trying to sell bagism as the next coolest thing for months but were having a hard time interesting anyone in spite of John's enormous celebrity.

Finally, it was John who broke the silence by asking me, "You don't happen to know of a good health food store nearby where we could get some decent macrobiotic food in a hurry? The food on the plane made me constipated."

I burst out laughing. I just hadn't expected constipation to be something people talked about with a god-idol-all-powerful celebrity.

He got the joke. He understood I was anxious. "Everyone's gotta crap," he said, laughing with me, not at me.

I told him about a health food store not far away just as Derek returned to the room. John gave Derek the name of the place and told him to try to get them to send over some macrobiotic food.

"Brown rice if they have it," John said.

Derek looked down at me. "Good. You two are getting along." He patted me on the shoulder. He glanced at his watch and said to John, "I'll come back shortly, and we'll start hanging the posters," and then he dashed through the door again, leaving John and me alone except for the ever-busy Nick and Mike, who were totally focused on arranging and testing camera, lighting, and sound equipment and running cables around the room.

This time as John and I continued to work, we talked. He wanted to know how I knew Derek and about California, New Jersey, and Montreal. For the second time that morning I was recounting my life to someone who seemed interested in it. I think I was the first war resister that John Lennon ever met.

"You did the right thing by coming to Canada and avoiding the draft," he said. "I would do the same."

I told him about my assignment for the *Sunday Express*. "Would you be willing to meet with a group of draft resisters and deserters?" I asked.

"Yes. Tell Derek to set it up."

As the starting time for the press conference drew nearer, the activity in the room grew more frantic. Yoko had been coming and going all morning, sometimes sitting with us and drawing a poster, telling John something, listening quietly to our conversation, seemingly studying me in a curious way, before dashing off again to what I knew by now were two other rooms connected to 1742. I had been sent on errands into both.

Yoko and Derek had been busy in the third room, interviewing a local Montreal nanny for Kyoko, Yoko's slim, dark-haired, dark-eyed, almost-six-year-old daughter. [28]

Kyoko was a nice touch for the Bed-In. She gave the show an air of a pajama party at the John and Yoko family home on a Sunday morning while pancakes were cooking on the stove.

I also discovered on my first errand that I was not the first gate crasher to the party. That award went to a tall, handsome Englishman, thirty-year-old Richard Glanville-Brown, a recent émigré to Montreal. He worked for Capital Records (Canada) as the promotion manager for Eastern Canada. Richard had heard on the radio the previous night around midnight that John and Yoko, accompanied by Kyoko and Derek Taylor, were coming to Montreal to hold a Bed-In. Richard had shown up at the hotel at eight in the morning and contacted Derek.

Richard told me afterward that Derek had been slightly testy at first, telling Richard, "If you're here for the glory I don't want you. If you're here to help, then I could use you."

For most of the first hour I had been there, Richard had manned the phone in the middle room, acting as Derek's second-in-command. He would be Derek's invaluable right-hand man for the rest of the Bed-In, not only as Derek's media backup but as the point man in charge of getting food and drink into the suite, calling in and sending away cleaning staff, and generally providing a very capable pair of extra hands.

The entire Lennon entourage arriving from the UK was a grand total of six people—John, Yoko, Kyoko, Derek, Nick, and Mike. There were no traveling secretaries, no advance men, no nanny. Derek was, in effect, orchestrating and managing the entire affair singlehandedly, with direction and suggestions from Yoko and John. That morning, the only additions to the inner circle had been Richard Glanville-Brown and me.

I was stunned by how few people were running the show.

I continued to fill in the bubble letters for "Peace," "Hair," and "Love."

John began to produce more drawings—large self-portraits and portraits of his and Yoko's heads and smaller nude, full-figure cartoons of their bodies. John wrote on one, "I love Yoko." Yoko saw this, knelt down between us and drew a similar nude cartoon self-portrait with the words, "I love John." It was amazing to see them talk to each other through their drawings.

Yoko dashed off to the other side of the room to help Derek, Mike, and Nick, who were starting to hang the finished posters with Scotch tape.

John made another drawing of Yoko and wrote below it, "We both married foreigners/forever."

The flowers and vases that Richard Glanville-Brown had ordered arrived, and Derek and Richard ran around the room placing huge vases of chrysanthemums in strategic locations before disappearing again into the middle room.

The walls still had plenty of room for more posters. John kept drawing. I kept filling in the letters until I finished all the filling in that I could. I was waiting for him to start another drawing when he turned to me and said, "Why don't you draw one?"

Wow, I thought, my one chance in a million to impress him.

I had been admiring the casual way he drew with very loose movements, lots of arm motion, very fluid, long strokes, often done quickly as if trying to get the most out of the fewest lines. He worked this way whether he was drawing faces or figures—minimalistic, flowing, round.

I wanted to copy what he was doing. I drew busts of Yoko and John holding hands on my poster board. It was my first try and it wasn't bad— the figures were easily recognizable as portraits of John and Yoko, but too minimalistic, too stiff, too sharp, and a little self-conscious. It didn't have the free-flowing qualities of John's or Yoko's hands.

The picture wasn't going to impress anyone, but I was still hoping that my words might fit in with their theme. I already knew what I wanted to say. *La guerre est finie.* It was the title of the Alain Resnais movie I had walked by dozens of times when it played at the local French-language movie house near my apartment. *La guerre est finie*—*The War Is Over*, or simply, *War Is Over*. It fit right in with the peace theme that John and Yoko were promoting.

I was quite pleased with myself.

I wrote it across the top of my poster and immediately realized I had a problem.

I couldn't remember whether the last word was spelled "*fini*" or "*finie.*"

I wrote it as "*fini*," and then wrote below my John and Yoko caricatures, "*Yoko et John*" and "*L' vie [sic] et l'amour*"—life and love. I had also misspelled *la vie*—life—but hadn't noticed.

Holding the poster up I stared at the upper line once more, trying to conjure up the movie house marquee and the correct spelling for "*finie.*"

John looked at my poster and asked me, "What's that?"

"*La guerre est finie,*" I told him, "It's French for 'the war is over.' Like we just declare the war over and walk away." I was describing what I had done.

He kept staring at the poster seemingly deep in thought.

"If we just give up the notion that war is inevitable, we could all live in peace," he said.

"It says 'life and love' at the bottom. My only problem is that I don't know whether *finie* has an 'e' on the end or not."

His eyebrows went up behind his glasses. He studied the poster and said, "I don't know how it's spelled either. There has to be someone who knows. There must be a French maid in the hallway." He was excited about what I had written. He stood and took the poster out of my hand. He went to the door and peeked into the hallway. I followed right behind.

The hallway was empty except for the security guard down the hall and the housekeeper in front of another room. John went into the hall in his pajamas and bare feet. I followed. He asked the housekeeper if she knew how to spell *finie*. She didn't speak French. She had no idea. John waved over the security guard, who also had no idea how to spell it.

Returning to the room, I reminded him that we were in Montreal and that much of the province spoke only French. Someone came up with the French word for peace—*paix*. John wrote this on a poster board along with the word "hair," in English since no one knew the French word for hair.

"The French are beautiful people," John said.

By this time, a new problem surfaced. The Scotch tape used to attach the posters to the walls began to peel, dropping the posters all around us, one at a time, no matter how much Scotch tape was applied. Derek phoned the front desk to locate some thumbtacks, but the hotel management ruled them out. They didn't want holes in the walls. Nick or Mike came up with the idea of using the gray gaffer tape in addition to the Scotch tape. This seemed to work better though only time would tell. The Scotch tape had also worked well at first.

Nick filmed Yoko and me taking turns trying to figure out how to make the posters stick to the walls. [29]

I talked briefly to Derek about setting something up with some war resisters. Derek liked the idea and said he would arrange a time.

With the press conference beginning soon, John, Derek, Yoko, Richard, Nick, Mike, and I all pitched in hanging John and Yoko's remaining posters on the walls and windows behind the bed, putting double and triple tape on some. I left my misspelled *La guerre est finie* poster aside, since everything else going up was either in John or Yoko's hand, but John found a place and hung my poster on the wall.

Cool, I thought, realizing it was the only thing on the walls not drawn by John or Yoko.

Cool, I thought, too, that I had thought up something that had gotten John's attention for a few moments. I never thought what I wrote would go any farther, though I clearly knew I would remember getting drawing lessons from John Lennon for a long time.

Finally, all was ready. John and Yoko pulled down the covers on the bed and hopped in. Nick and Mike made last-minute adjustments to their equipment. I stood to one side while Derek went to the door to let in the press, which by then had been lined up down the hallway and into the middle room for about ten or fifteen minutes. Kyoko was safely tucked away in the third room to the south playing with her new best friend, the young local nanny.

And my day is only half over, I thought, checking my watch and reminding myself that at some point I needed to head downstairs and check in with Ivan Sanderson about finding film clips of flying saucers and Abominable Snowmen.

CHAPTER 39

To ANYONE WHO came through the door to the Bed-In, I clearly belonged, though it was unclear how I fit in. I was neither working the film equipment, lying under the covers, nor working the press like Derek and Richard were. Johnny Vader arrived with a small entourage from the Globe. Johnny and I exchanged secret glances. Colin Gravenor, with a couple of staffers from the *Sunday Express*, looked perplexed as he edged behind the crowd of twenty or thirty reporters and asked me, "How did you get in before everyone else?"

"Derek Taylor's an old friend of mine from Los Angeles. I'm going to line up a meeting with John and Yoko and some draft resisters and deserters later in the week. It should make a good story."

"You did well." He smiled and patted me on the back before turning his attention to John and Yoko as they began to field questions about the purpose of their mission, their ideas on peace, their latest album, bagism, and how they liked Canada.

Even in the first hour of the first press conference, I saw a disconnect between what the media wanted and what the Lennons were selling. The media wanted a Beatles' story.

John and Yoko dodged questions about the Beatles and peddled the idea of peace, naked honesty, settling differences without bloodshed, and loving each other and ourselves more than hating someone else. All these themes had been rippling through the ether for years. John and Yoko were talking about the idea of marketing peace like a commodity, selling it like soap. Push the idea of peace into the headlines; push war out, they said.

The Bed-In was supposed to be an alternative to large mass rallies that had increasingly been turning into battlegrounds between protestors and police. Yoko and John were telling everyone to go home, protest in bed instead. Avoid violence.

From the moment it started, the Bed-In was hard work. John and Yoko had to answer question after question about what they were trying to achieve. Though John seemed to be able to easily turn most of the questions into humor, I also sensed an underlying edginess, maybe a touch of frustration at some of the more skeptical questions or questions that dragged the discussion away from the Bed-In and back to the Beatles and their music.

John kept deflecting questions about the Beatles. The campaign for peace was entirely a John and Yoko show, and not a Beatles' event. It felt like John was trying to rewire the psyche of the entire press corps to stop focusing on the Beatles.

The new anti-war theme intrigued me. Had the Beatles ever overtly campaigned against the war before? Their music had been peaceful and loving, but before Yoko, I couldn't remember any of the Beatles being actively anti-war. John Lennon was clearly charting a new direction for himself separate from the Beatles.

From my perspective, I also saw no sign of the rumors that Yoko was the Svengali behind the new John. If John had now become someone different than he had been as a member of the Beatles in an intellectual and creative sense, I had to believe he wanted to go there, and Yoko, from what I could see, was the perfect complement to what he wanted to do with his life beyond the Beatles. It was John who gave the memorable quotes, who was in charge, and who understood better than anyone the power of his celebrity. Yoko seemed to me to be his echo, maybe even his biggest fan, trying to explain what John had just said. John appeared to be looking after Yoko, providing her with openings to fill, supporting her, trying to push her forward on stage.

Interacting with the press was clearly no fun. After Derek ushered out the first group of reporters and let in the second group, they began asking the same tedious questions.

I remained for only a few questions and answers and then tried to quietly slip out. Derek stopped me before I got to the hallway and asked, "You're coming back later, aren't you? I'd like to see you. We still haven't talked, and I still haven't given you a date for your draft resisters."

"What would be a good time?"

"Whenever you want. You were a great help, Joseph. John thought you were a great help. We can talk later this afternoon, maybe five or six o'clock should be good. We should be winding down by then. You're always welcome. I should go back now," he said, glancing over his shoulder at the room full of media people.

Amazing guy, I thought as I headed downstairs. I was in awe of how he seemed to be managing the entire show by himself. I felt good being invited back anytime.

Downstairs, Ivan was delighted to see me. Discovering I hadn't had any lunch, he ordered sandwiches and another pot of coffee from room service. Instead of getting right to work, he made me go over everything I had seen and heard upstairs.

He was eager to hear every detail. I definitely enjoyed the attention, and I liked making him laugh when I told him about how John had gotten constipated on airplane food.

Guy, the freelance film director for our film loop, stopped by in the middle of the afternoon while Ivan was on the phone. Guy was a slight, blond-haired Québécois artist about my age with an easy-going manner and an eclectic interest in politics, space, Tarzan, and film noir. We bonded right away when he said he was looking for a low-budget film noir feature script and I told him about the treatment I was working on.

The three of us talked about the unexplained. We were all open-minded, agreeing that flying saucers or spaceships could be buzzing around earth. Unusual forms of life—even Abominable Snowmen and Loch Ness Monsters—might also exist in remote areas.

"And don't forget," Ivan said cheerfully, "if there are Abominable Snowmen, Abominable Snow-women and Snow-children must exist too." The same had to be true of Loch Ness Monsters, we all agreed. We talked a little about what might be discovered on the moon. The first attempt to land a man on the moon was to take place in two months.

Guy explained what he expected to do with the footage once we gathered it. An hour later, he took off to another meeting, leaving Ivan and me alone again.

Finally, Ivan and I got to work, calling lists of telephone numbers he had put together, trying to track down any and all footage of unexplained phenomena.

I was surprised to learn the number of places UFOs, Big Foot-type man-apes, and Loch Ness-type sea monsters had been spotted in recent and ancient times. Ivan—he insisted I call him that—was an encyclopedia of the unexplained. He had leads on the location of a number of well-known film clips of purported sightings of unexplained creatures and objects. We had to make scores of phone calls to dozens of countries to locate each snippet of film, find the legal owners, and then negotiate for the rights to use it in the Strange, Strange World exhibit.

Ivan simply shrugged off false leads and kept going, never discouraged, and always cheerful, insisting on long breaks for more coffee while we waited for our contacts to return calls.

I told him at one point that I thought he looked familiar, and he explained that he had often appeared on television with exotic animals on a variety of programs, most notably, *The Garry Moore Show*. I had seen him there. He was one of the first scientists to show live, exotic animals on TV. He was a genuine scientist—a naturalist with what was called in the UK a Tripos from Cambridge University, a degree in zoology, botany, and geology. He also studied anthropology and pre-history. He had traveled the world extensively, leading scientific expeditions in his teens and twenties, writing a number of scientific nature classics of journeys to Africa, the Caribbean, and Central America, illustrating the books himself. [30]

When he was still at Cambridge, Ivan had coined the term "cryptozoology" to refer to the study of crypto (Greek for hidden) animals known through stories, legends, and scientifically unverified modern sightings. [31]

Ivan wrote his crossover book, *The Abominable Snowman*, in 1961. Though he had dabbled in the world of strange creatures and phenomena previously, this book marked his almost complete immersion into the unexplained. [32]

The time flew by as we talked on the phone and I listened to his tales.

Around four-thirty, he looked at his watch and announced, "We've done enough for today."

"You're sure?" I asked, feeling guilty that we had done so little.

"We have plenty of time. You should be heading upstairs. You have an article to write. I have a few other things to take care of. Besides, I'm curious about what's going on. I'll want a full report tomorrow. See you in the morning."

What a generous guy, I thought as I headed upstairs again.

CHAPTER 40

BY LATE AFTERNOON, the Bed-In had settled into a chaotic routine. Derek had more or less scheduled groups of media people, carefully selected fans, and celebrities on the hour, half hour, or quarter hour. Those waiting for their chance to enter the inner sanctum were cleared downstairs, then cleared again outside the elevators, and then lined up outside in the hall, sometimes standing, sometimes seated on chairs along the corridor. A very select few of those waiting were briefly let into the middle room with Derek's okay to wait for their audience.

The only people who were allowed to stay behind were visitors that Derek or John thought were particularly interesting or useful in some way. They included a few of the photographers, reporters, and others like me who had some special connection to Derek or John or who they selected on the spot. As a result, the number of people hanging around in the main room and in the middle room increased as time went on although in the scheme of things those who were able to come and go through the week-long Bed-In never amounted to more than a few dozen people in total.

Most of the reporters who had arrived for the first press conference came from the local print media. More radio and TV reporters with their cameras, microphones, and assistants followed during the afternoon. Media people from outside the Montreal area also arrived by car, train, bus, and plane from other parts of Canada and the US. Ordinary fans and celebrities alike showed up or phoned from North America and Europe.

The contrast between the quiet period, which I had shared earlier in the morning with John, Yoko, and Derek, and the media frenzy that followed made an impact on me. The room now felt more like an office. John seemed more energized but also more businesslike. Derek, too, seemed more focused, more methodical, though whenever he saw me he gave me a warm smile and said something soothing, almost as if I was somehow part of his reality check. More than once he asked me what I thought of the show in general or of a particular interview.

The Bed-In was the first real media event I'd witnessed. I wasn't sure what to think. When I told this to Derek, he said, "Give me your first impressions."

"It feels somewhat unreal, like everything's being manufactured. Everything comes down to the same questions over and over again."

"Exactly," he said with a smile. "And it's like this all the time wherever John goes."

I was becoming less infatuated with overwhelming fame as each minute went by.

John, too, was friendly but more distant and always preoccupied, always marshalling his strength and wit to be *on* with the media and everyone else who seemed to want to talk to him.

From John I sensed a toughness, an abrasiveness, an edge of aggression, but also a funny, warm, vulnerable person underneath, aware of his power, determined to try to use it in a positive way—meaning, I think, in a willful way, to *have* his way. At the same time, he was actually trying to reach out and touch the people within sight of him.

Yoko's main focus always appeared to be John. I felt, at times, like she was his guardian angel, at other times, like she was his understudy, and at still other times, like she was sitting back, studying John and to a lesser extent studying everyone in the room from afar.

She was thirty-six, twelve years older than me. Most of the time, she seemed like the oldest person in the room. John Lennon was only a few months older than my brother. I was used to people his age. Derek Taylor was thirteen years older than me and a year older than Yoko but much younger seemingly in my mind. Yoko seemed almost like a parental figure, reserved, not really unfriendly but not what I would call friendly either.

Feeling uncomfortable just standing around and watching, I asked Derek if I could do anything.

"Why don't you take a turn on the phone?" he suggested, leading me into the middle room. I sat in the chair beside the bed, answered the phone, and took messages.

On my second or third call, I picked up the phone and said something like, "Bed-In Headquarters, can I help you?"

"This is Allen Ginsberg," I heard the familiar voice of America's poet prince on the other end of the line. "I'd like to speak with John Lennon."

"Allen," I said, very excited. "It's Joseph. Jay Thompson's friend. We met when you were visiting the University of Southern California."

I was hoping if Derek remembered me, Allen Ginsberg might, too.

Dead silence.

I went on. "I delivered a message from Jay that your photos were ready. We ended up spending a couple of hours talking." Two years before, in Los Angeles, celebrity photographer and friend, Jay Thompson, the same person who had introduced me to Paul Krassner, had taken some photos of Ginsberg for a book he was producing on the counterculture. Jay found out I was meeting Ginsberg and told me to tell him his photos were ready. Ginsberg and I spent a couple hours later that evening smoking his grass and my bananadine. He drew a picture of the Buddha's footprint and gave it to me.

More silence.

"You still there?" I asked.

"What are you doing there?" he finally asked, sounding suspicious.

"Montreal seemed like a better idea than Vietnam."

He chuckled. I explained I was helping Derek, John, and Yoko.

"Can I talk to John?"

"Let me see. He's giving an interview in the other room."

I found John and Yoko deep in conversation with a reporter hovering over the bed holding a microphone between John and Yoko while a camera guy filmed the scene.

Derek was standing alone against the wall, thoughtfully following the interview.

I whispered to Derek, "Allen Ginsberg's on the line and wants to talk to John."

"Get his number. Tell him John will call him back. Or Allen can call later. Tell him to call after six. John will definitely want to speak to him. Tell him to come to Montreal if he can."

I returned to the phone and relayed the message.

Ginsberg asked me. "What's the scene like?"

I described the comings and goings as best I could. He gave me his phone number and told me he'd wait to hear from John or try calling back.

At six, Derek ended the formal media interviews, and the main bedroom turned into a cocktail party for the handful of select media people and others who were permitted to stay. John and Yoko, sometimes from the bed, sometimes milling around the room, talked to everyone. Other times, John talked on the phone. I wandered around, making small talk with the others, getting to know how they happened to be there.

Yoko disappeared to look after Kyoko in the far room, and I finally got some chat time with Derek. We talked for a few minutes about his wife and kids who I'd met in LA and were now back in England. The hard part for me was talking about old friends like Mike Vosse and David Anderle, the two people Derek and I knew in common. David was at Elektra records in charge of A&R, working with The Doors, Nico, Tim Buckley, and Judy Collins. Mike was working as an A&R man and house freak for A&M records where he was instrumental in luring the Flying Burrito Brothers to the label.

"I miss those days and all those good people," Derek said.

"Me, too." I gave him a weak smile.

"Don't worry," he added as if reading my mind. "This war can't go on forever. You'll be able to go home one day."

I wasn't so sure I wanted to go back, but I thought I would like the freedom to visit one day.

Derek asked me what I had been doing since he had last seen me in LA. I told him about my checkered history with the poster king, the think tank, the tabloids, and my current uncertain future. "If you can think of anything I can do for Apple, just let me know," I said, immediately regretting this. "I'm sorry. I shouldn't have said that. Everyone's hitting on you for something."

He laughed. "You don't have to apologize. It's John Lennon and the Beatles. They never stop hearing people asking them for something. But that's also how they find the right people to help them. It's a two-way street. John likes you. Leave it with me. Let me think about it. Maybe I can come up with something. In the meantime, let's figure out a time to meet with the draft resisters and deserters."

As much as I wanted to write the article, the thought of putting together a representative cross-section of draft resisters and deserters was already making me anxious.

CHAPTER 41

JOHN LENNON WAS giving the draft resisters and deserters a rare full hour on Thursday afternoon. Derek was leaving the content and players completely up to me.

What did John want, I asked myself. Just as I had wanted to impress him when I drew my *La guerre est finie* poster, I felt the same obligation to find a good crew to meet with him.

Wasn't the whole point to use celebrity to promote peace?

I tried thinking of how to build on John's idea. Did I even know any newsworthy draft resisters or deserters? I wanted both categories of war resister to be there. Finding the right draft resisters would be challenging. For most war resisters, including me, draft resisting was never a full-time job. Most of the ones I knew had made a point of trying to put the past behind them and blend into the Canadian landscape and culture. Finding deserters would be even harder. Deserters were the rarest of the war resister breed. For every twenty draft resisters, probably no more than one deserter had gone to Canada. Getting into Canada and becoming a landed immigrant had been much more difficult for them.

Since Canada had no draft, resisting conscription wasn't illegal. As long as the other requirements for immigration were met, the official policy was to welcome draft evaders. But Canada had its own armed forces. Desertion was a serious crime. Anyone who had been sworn into the armed forces in the US was under the jurisdiction of military law and not the civilian courts. Canada had been struggling with its policy toward US military deserters long before I'd arrived. While draft resisters were able to apply for work status at points of entry (or from inside the country as I had) and could lead normal lives in the open in Canada once they became landed immigrants, until a few weeks before the Bed-In, deserters were more restricted. Canadian immigration officers were allowed to use their discretion on whether to permit a US deserter to apply for landed immigrant status at points of entry. Rather than risk being turned down at the border, many US military deserters had simply entered as tourists and gone underground inside Canada, often living under pseudonyms and working off the books. [33] Word on the street in Canada at the time was that at least one underground network was smuggling deserters to Cuba, Sweden, and elsewhere in Europe before the RCMP could track them down and deport them.

An equal number of rumors were floating around that the FBI and CIA employed informants in Montreal and elsewhere in the country to look for deserters and report them to the Canadian authorities, who, in turn, would boot them out for overstaying their visit.

Then, just weeks before the Bed-In, the year-old Canadian government under Prime Minister Trudeau finally made its policy clear—US military deserters were to be treated like all other immigrants. If they applied at the border or an airport entry point, they were to be given temporary working papers and then, landed immigrant status if they qualified. In the ensuing weeks before the Bed-In a handful of deserters living underground had surfaced inside Canada and applied for landed immigrant status. Several hundred more had shown up at points of entry—not exactly a flood, but at least I now had the possibility of rounding up a few.

I headed to the bars after leaving the Bed-In early that evening, looking for draft resisters and deserters to present to John and Yoko.

The first place I went was the Don Juan, the oldest of Johnny Vago's three bars. I was looking for the manager, Ben Apfelbaum, a friend and fellow draft resister who had arrived in Canada a few months before me. The Don Juan was starting to fill up with dancers and drinkers. Ben wasn't there. Someone thought he might be at the Pub.

A big guy with black frizzy hair and beard, a larger than life personality, and a degree in anthropology, he always had something to say about politics. I thought it would be fun to watch him interact with John Lennon. [34]

Ben wasn't at the Pub or next door at the Boiler Room. I ran into Johnny Vago, the owner of the Pub, the Boiler Room, and the Don Juan, and asked him if he knew any interesting draft resisters or deserters who I could interview for a story I was working on. I didn't mention John Lennon for fear that I would be swamped with people trying to get into the Bed-In.

Vago suggested Stephen, a musician and former McGill University student who was waiting tables in the Boiler Room. Stephen was from New York, of draft age, and against the war, but it turned out he had a deferment and wasn't a draft resister.

I had a beer and inserted myself into several different crowds, listening to what people were saying about the Bed-In.

No one was talking about it.

Interesting, I thought. Inside the Bed-In at the Queen Elizabeth Hotel all the media attention made the event feel like the center of the universe. Outside, a dozen blocks away, it wasn't important. When I mentioned the Bed-In I got more cynicism than I expected. "What the fuck does it have to do with me?" one guy asked me, and another said, "It's a publicity stunt." A writer friend of mine carped, "John Lennon's the guy you'd never lend ten dollars to, because you'd never get it back."

When I posed the question another way, "Would you pass up the chance to meet John Lennon?" the mood changed. "Only if I could talk with him alone, one-on-one," one person said. Everyone else simply said yes. He was a Beatle. The Beatles had crossed the Atlantic and given us permission to laugh again in the weeks following the assassination of President Kennedy. John, the leading force in the Beatles, had snake charmed us. He had blown our minds with otherworldly psychedelic rock songs on albums like *Rubber Soul, Revolver, Sgt. Pepper's Lonely Hearts Club Band*, and the rest.

I could have found a hundred people to drag to the Bed-In, but I needed bona fide draft resisters and deserters.

"If you're interested in what's going on at the Bed-In, you should talk to Ben. He was there," Alan, the bartender, told me, "He knows Yoko somehow."

Now, I definitely had to talk with Ben to compare notes.

I returned to the Don Juan. The disco was a step up for Ben. He had been the manager of the Pub and Boiler Room when they first opened, but now he was not only managing the Don Juan but was one of Vago's junior partners. [35]

By the time I arrived, the music was blaring and strobe lights were bouncing around the main room, giving the Don Juan a noisy, psychedelic atmosphere. Just about everyone smoked cigarettes. The ventilation in the basement suite was never good. A blue haze hovered everywhere.

Ben was there, dressed in a loose white two-piece suit, looking like a taller, younger version of Allen Ginsberg with a bushier head of hair.

He greeted me warmly. We had been friends since the Globe Christmas Party where Joe Azaria had introduced us. Ben was the *Sunday Express's* first book reviewer.

"I heard you were at the Bed-In," I said. I had to shout over the music to be heard.

He rolled his eyes, laughed, and shouted back. "What a circus."

"How'd you get in?" I asked.

"I know Yoko from New York when she was doing her thing there. I just talked my way in." Always on his toes, he stopped our conversation to tell one of the waiters to look after some customers in the far corner. Then, to me, he said, grinning, "Come to the office. I want to show you something. You'll appreciate it."

I followed him to the office in back. He shut the door behind us to block the noise. From the floor behind the desk, he lifted a large picture frame and turned it to face me.

It was a white poster board with the caricature drawing in felt-tip marker of John and Yoko in John's hand with the word "Bagism" sprawled across it.

"I just got it framed. What do you think?"

"Pretty cool."

"I told Yoko and John that I needed something to promote their cause in my club. I said I was going to dedicate one of the rooms to world peace." He laughed and rolled his eyes again to make sure I got the joke. "Actually, I'm going to hang it in the little room and call it the Bag Room—whatever that's supposed to mean."

"I was there, too." I thought I could trust him. I told him about my current mission to try to find a representative group of draft resisters and deserters for Thursday afternoon.

"Would you be one?" I asked.

He rocked his head from side to side. "I don't really think so. I've already been there. I don't want to go back. Thursday afternoon's bad for me anyway. I have an appointment with a lawyer for George."

George was a young draft resister who had been crashing off and on at Ben's place. George had gotten busted for possession of marijuana. Ben had been trying to keep him out of jail and from being deported. George was definitely out of the question as far as I was concerned.

Ben couldn't think of any other names either, which was surprising. Since he knew so many people, I was starting to worry even more.

Returning to my place, I tried putting together a list of interesting draft resisters I had crossed paths with who might make good copy for my story. An actor who had done a few beer commercials and had come to Canada a year before me told me that he was erasing all ties to the past. He had no interest in talking about the draft or the old country. An eighteen-year-old kid sent to Montreal by his San Francisco-New York-Paris beatnik parents to the home of an artist friend had left Montreal months before for Paris. Once he realized that dishwasher was the only job he seemed qualified for in Montreal, he decided he might as well head to France to wash dishes there.

I dialed the number of Tom, the black war resister who lived with the heavyset blond-haired woman in the student ghetto when I lived on Aylmer Street. I hadn't seen him for nearly a year and a half. He was no longer at the number I dialed. His girlfriend said they'd broken up the year before. She had no idea where he was.

The only staff member at The Globe Newspaper Group at the time who was a bona fide draft resister was probably the person I knew least well. I didn't bother calling him, mainly because I already knew from Johnny that any public association with me could get him fired.

Finally, I called John the Photographer, a draft resister and freelancer who occasionally shot pictures for *Midnight* and the other tabloids. John the Photographer was also one of several freelancers who contributed occasionally to the underground paper *Logos*.

"As long as I can take photos, count me in," he told me as soon as I explained what I wanted.

"You can take all the photos you want," I told him.

More important, he agreed to help hunt down a few more draft resisters and deserters for me and set up a meeting.

All I could do was hope for the best since I had to work the next day with Ivan, hunting down more film footage.

At least I had one draft resister. It was a start. Stories, of course, abounded that all the major cities in Canada were flooded with draft resisters and deserters by then, but the truth was far, far fewer of us had made the trek to Canada than the rumors suggested. Canada's immigration records would back this up years later.

CHAPTER 42

EARLY THE NEXT morning, Wednesday, May 28, the second day of the Bed-In, I again started the day in the Queen Elizabeth Hotel at Ivan's side. I worked on the phone and chatted with Ivan all morning. [36]

I told him I had been part of several hoaxes involving UFOs and alien spacemen at *Midnight*. He was familiar with many of the stories appearing in the Globe's tabloids.

"Those stories aren't all bad," he explained. "On one hand, they discredit the serious investigations of these phenomena. But on the other hand, they keep the interest alive in the public's mind. The more people think about these things the better."

He thought that the field discoveries would most likely come first from the public as they had in the past. He had published "Wisconsin's Abominable Snowman" in April and "The Missing Link?" about the Minnesota Iceman in May in the adventure magazine, *Argosy*. [37]

I wanted all the craziness to be true. I wanted the world to find other worlds or long-lost living creatures that could take us backward or forward in time and space. I was for anything that would give the whole world a shake by the shoulders and yell in our collective ears, "Stop war, stop killing."

Thou shalt not kill.

Ten fucking Commandments, I thought, and we can't even collectively agree on believing in even one of them.

CHAPTER 43

IVAN SANDERSON LIKED to take long breaks and knock off early so he could work on other projects he had on the go. So, I found myself popping in and out of the Bed-In on a regular basis before, between, and after my short sessions with him.

I was expecting to see something different each time I arrived at the Bed-In, but with few exceptions, it was more of the same. John and Yoko were repeating each other's lines so often it became difficult to tell who said what.

John could sound tough and angry in some of his responses. At other times, he spoke with a very quiet soothing voice and seemed quite at ease. When I had been alone with him, I sensed a genuine calm and relaxed human being. Now, he was at work, at the office conducting business like a serious businessman, but he was enjoying it.

Whatever anyone else thought of Yoko, John clearly loved being with her. It was the kind of relationship I dreamed of—finding a creative partner, someone who I could spend the day at work with, go to interesting places together, and go home at night and sleep with, something John couldn't do with the other Beatles.

Someone asked John whether or not he was still smoking marijuana. He claimed he had found a new way to get high.

Yoko insisted they got high on love.

One reporter laughed out loud.

They both said a pure macrobiotic diet of tea and brown rice would get you high.

When John suggested everyone should just love everything and everyone, Yoko suggested that everyone should just go home and make a poster or draw a flower.

✷ ✷ ✷

I noticed that in addition to my poster, La guerre est fini [sic], still on the wall, a few drawings by Kyoko had also been hung, the only other drawings in the suite that hadn't been made by John or Yoko. My contribution still held the record for the most misspellings on a single poster.

Journalist Beverley Mitchell wrote about my poster along with several others in her Montreal Star article on Wednesday.

✷ ✷ ✷

Derek was calm and cool on the outside, always friendly and warm to me, but always vigilant, keeping an eye on everything and everyone and always ready to deal with anything John or Yoko needed.

Derek continued to fascinate me, in some ways, even more than John and Yoko. John and Yoko were always on, always ready to be in the spotlight, always ready to try to convince someone in the room or on the phone that peace and love were better than war, that non-violence was better than violence no matter what the circumstances, but they also had the almost constant attention and often adulation to spur them on.

Derek received little to no adulation. He had power over who came and went, but it was never about him or his ego. His constant focus was simply on whether the business of the Bed-In was running smoothly. He was the hip corporate guy—the consummate man-behind-the-scenes, all seeing, all knowing, all caring for everyone else.

At one point, he slid up beside me while I was watching an interview and said, "Keep your eyes and ears open for anything suspicious."

"In what way?" I asked.

"We know we're being infiltrated. RCMP, FBI, and CIA. They're all interested in whatever John does. They're all watching him."

I felt a shiver go up my spine.

Whether or not the peace message was getting through, John Lennon was camped out nearly on the border with the US, spurring on America's anti-war peaceniks and various other rebels. Lennon's in-your-face message was something new. It was propaganda, not from some sovereign nation but from an individual, a pop star, someone who could command an audience of news outlets at will.

Lennon was openly protesting the US government's decision to prevent him from entering the country. He was a criminal in the eyes of the US government, something that I could relate to since I was wanted by the FBI. For the moment, I was part of the criminal Beatle bandito gang. [38] It made me feel even closer to him. It also struck me as ironic that if he had been an American, his drug bust would have gotten him out of the draft.

Having been under surveillance myself by the FBI and RCMP, I had no trouble believing the RCMP, FBI, and CIA were interested in the inner workings of the Bed-In. It had become a magnet not only for American radicals and counterculture types but for Canadian radicals, including some serious Québécois separatists who, at one point, tried arguing with John that violence was a necessary means to an end. John held his ground, arguing that violence was never justified. Period. I liked that.

I helped out once again by manning one of the phone lines in the middle room, and, at one point, found myself talking to Allen Ginsberg a second time.

"What's happening? Who's there?" he asked.

Once again, I described the scene as best I could of John and Yoko in bed talking to reporters or on the telephone; the strong scent of incense filling the air; and a local group of about twenty Hari Krishnas with shaved heads and wearing saffron-colored robes dancing, chanting, blowing sea shell horns, and clapping finger cymbals at the foot of the bed.

"Come on up. It's your scene," I insisted.

"I'm thinking about it," Allen told me.

I phoned John the Photographer several times during the day. He had located a few more draft resisters and deserters. We were to meet at one of their houses later that evening. Before heading home, I had a quick drink with Derek in the bar on the ground floor.

"You provide a good excuse to get away from the intensity of the Bed-In for a little while," he said. He asked me how the meeting with the draft resisters was going. I told him I was working on it. I was thankful he didn't press me for details.

"We'll go out in a night or two and have a proper dinner," he insisted. I realized in some strange way I was helping him stay grounded.

Except for John the Photographer, the only other person I knew in the gathering of potentially acceptable resisters and deserters that evening was Grant, a quiet, thoughtful deserter, who I had occasionally run into at the office of the underground paper *Logos*.

As a deserter from the military, Grant had been living a shadowy underground life for the past year. He had a wife and a six-month-old daughter, who had been born when he was stateless in Canada. His life had changed dramatically three weeks before the Bed-In when the government policy on deserters had been clarified. He had just received his working papers and was waiting to get approval for his landed immigrant status. I was happy for him, as I had lived in the same shadowy world for my first five months in Canada. Being stateless for any length of time took an emotional toll.

I wasn't so happy to learn that half of the fifteen or twenty people gathered that night weren't draft resisters or deserters but Canadians who wanted to meet John Lennon.

When I said that only the draft resisters, deserters, spouses, and Grant's baby could go, several of the others turned against me and wanted to put it to a vote.

"You don't represent us," one of the more militant non-draft resisters told me.

"And none of you represent me," I said. "Look at us. A handful of people who claim to represent the Montreal and Canadian draft resisters and deserters, and we can't draw enough of us here to fill this small living room."

We were a ragtag collection of Americans who came to Canada from such different backgrounds and for so many different reasons that the only thing we had in common was the single act of defiance against the war.

When one of the resisters started talking about Marxist-Leninist protocol, I wanted to scream. Someone else talked about the irrelevance of peace at a time when the US was a boiling cauldron of violence.

"The only way to meet violence is through violence," another of these self-styled "anti-war" warmongers chimed in.

Our little group was pretty typical. Most of us just wanted to get along in the world. Only a few were militant, but they were on the verge of hijacking the rest of us. The militants were definitely not representative of me or most of the other draft resisters in the country who wanted to quietly disappear into the Canadian mosaic.

I was on the verge of calling the whole thing off. The last thing I wanted was to arrive at the Bed-In with a bunch of people in total discord.

Somehow I managed to keep cool. I didn't have time to go hunting for other draft resisters and deserters. And they needed me to get into the Bed-In. I sensed that all of them were more interested in basking in the glow of John Lennon's celebrity than starting a fight.

The commercial instincts of John the Photographer trumped what sympathy he might have had for the militants. "Look, this is an opportunity for all of us. Let's leave it at that. Joseph set this up so some draft resisters and deserters could meet John and Yoko."

Thankfully, most of the others agreed, and the rest fell in line.

In the end, we weren't going as a strident group of American anti-war protestors, but as ordinary Americans who had simply chosen a peaceful way to protest the war—by removing ourselves from the war machine, *by declaring: the war is over.*

La guerre est finie pour nous, pour moi.

Everyone finally agreed that only the draft resisters and deserters could go, along with the two spouses and Grant's baby. We weren't a formal group. We didn't need an agenda. Even though in the end, everyone agreed I was nominally in charge, I told them, "I won't script you in any way. You can say what you want once you get there."

My mission was to produce the players, sit back, observe, and write an article about draft resisters, deserters, John Lennon, and Yoko Ono. By the time the gathering broke up, I was satisfied that I had enough draft resisters and deserters for the meeting. But as I walked home that night, something was still bothering me. I kept thinking about the concept of who represented me and what I believed. Might there be some value in creating some sort of group that could be more representative of the peace and love movement? Was the John Lennon-Yoko Ono Bed-In possibly a reawakening of the lost spirit of the hope I had felt in the spring and summer of 1967—the Summer of Love?

I also had to remind myself that the Bed-In was a business proposition for John and Yoko. They were selling peace and themselves. I was orchestrating the business of putting a disparate group of rebels together to feed into John and Yoko's business plan.

Like it or not, everything was business it seemed, even lofty ideals.

CHAPTER 44

I WORKED BRIEFLY with Ivan early the next morning, Thursday, May 29, the third day of the Bed-In. I told him about the previous day, including how repetitive John and Yoko were sounding and my difficulties with finding a presentable group of draft resisters and deserters.

In the course of our brief session I mentioned what Derek had said about infiltrators from the RCMP, FBI, and CIA.

He smiled. "I hope no one's taking any drugs."

"I doubt it." I thought John and Yoko were probably being extra careful about drugs. John wanted a visa for the US. Another drug bust wouldn't help.

Ivan let me go after an hour. He said he needed to work on one of his other projects. We were pretty close to getting all the footage we needed anyway.

I returned to the Bed-In midmorning, several hours before my draft resisters and deserters were supposed to arrive.

The main Bed-In room by then had become seedy, maybe not to someone who was seeing it for the first time, and probably not to anyone who was totally captivated by the magic of the Lennons, but having seen the place from the beginning, I couldn't help noticing that the chrysanthemums were drooping. Many of the posters had fallen down, been stepped on, and re-taped to the walls, often in different places, often with more than one kind of tape. The floor looked like a giant ashtray, littered with cigarette butts, crumpled messages, and dead flowers that had been brought as peace offerings by visitors.

The air conditioning wasn't working properly. Sweat, the lingering scent of incense, and the always-present cigarette smoke gave the room a funky smell.

Some of the old posters had disappeared, given away to fans, media personalities, and celebrities who stopped by. New posters had been drawn by John or Yoko and put up in their place. My *La guerre est fini [sic]* poster was still there along with a couple of drawings by Kyoko—the only other art on the walls not drawn by John or Yoko.

I caught Derek between phone calls and told him I had the draft resisters and deserters lined up and ready to go for two o'clock.

"We're already running late," Derek told me. "I hope your people won't mind waiting."

"They'll be fine," I assured him.

Along with the general scruffiness, the Bed-In appeared to me to have grown more businesslike, and the suite, more office-like. John and Yoko had settled into a routine as groups of media, fans, and celebrities arrived, sometimes for a few minutes, sometimes for a half hour or more, before being led out.

"Keep an eye out for anyone looking suspicious," Derek told me again, always on the lookout for the suspected RCMP, FBI, and CIA infiltrators.

Who didn't look suspicious, I wondered. Would undercover cops and spies come dressed in suits and ties, or would they more likely look like freaks? Was it possible that one of the draft resisters or deserters I had invited to the suite might be a spy or an undercover agent?

I tried not to think about that and stayed focused on the message.

Regardless of the audience, the message continued to be the same— peace, peace, peace, love, love, love, peace, peace, peace. John kept invoking Gandhi as the model. I wished someone would invoke Henry David Thoreau, too. Thoreau had invented modern civil disobedience. Gandhi had invoked Thoreau.

"Down with snobbery," Yoko railed. "Peace is for everyone." She sounded angry at the "hippies," claiming they were "snobs" and that they thought peace and love were only for themselves.

My little party of outlaws—four deserters, three draft resisters, two wives, one baby, and two people who shouldn't have been part of the group—assembled in the middle room a half an hour before two. Everyone was well groomed and dressed in their cleanest, nicest clothes.

Grant's baby was a bit restless, but Grant and his wife were tenderly looking after her. Of the two who didn't belong, one stowaway was another freelance photographer from *Logos*—a Canadian—who had attached himself to the group. I could have tossed him out for not being an American draft resister or deserter, but he was a nice kid. I'd seen him around the underground paper. He was so terrified I'd throw him out he wouldn't make eye contact with me until I finally told him, "As long as you just take photos and keep in the background, you're welcome to stay." The other stowaway was my friend, El, the tough-talking, dark-eyed Brit who owned the coffeehouse where I used to sing on amateur night. He had also snuck in with my crowd. I didn't have the heart to throw him out. Even if I tried, I wasn't sure he would go. Besides, the joker in me wondered what kind of draft resister John Lennon would think he was with his unmistakable British accent if he opened his mouth during our session with the Lennons. I didn't bother to tell El to keep quiet. I knew it would be a waste of time.

I explained that our audience with John and Yoko was running a little behind schedule but not to worry.

I left my party of dissidents in the middle room and returned to the Bed-In.

Yet again, John and Yoko were explaining how the Bed-In was like an ongoing advertising campaign, a celebrity endorsement for peace, just like a celebrity endorsement for soap. It reminded me in a way of telethons run by comedian Jerry Lewis to raise money for muscular dystrophy.

Returning to the middle room, I discovered Richard Glanville-Brown had called room service, and a cart with drinks had arrived for the draft resisters and deserters. The members of my entourage were nervous, but no one was complaining about the delay.

I returned to the Bed-In room through the connecting door and listened to more peace, more invocations to grow hair, more exhortations to stay in bed, have sex—anything but resorting to violence. John cleared his throat more often than he did at the start of the Bed-In. I wondered if his voice would hold up.

He sounded strident, insistent, almost bossy when anyone suggested causes existed that were worth fighting for.

No, no, no.

Peace, peace, peace.

Soap, soap, soap.

I was earning a master's degree in public relations and marketing without knowing it as I watched one of the most focused marketing campaigns in the history of advertising and promotion.

Derek, John, and Yoko, with minimal assistance from a handful of others like Richard Glanville-Brown and me, had created arguably the world's longest running press conference and one of the most intense and oversubscribed publicity campaigns in the history of print and electronic media. It had been achieved with little more than a few phones, poster boards, felt-tip markers, and John's celebrity. John and Yoko were cross-branding their products and images with peace. It was so simple, so elegant.

It was also compellingly interesting to see that no amount of celebrity could sell a lame product like bagism. The idea of peace connected in a visceral way with everyone. It was a hot brand. Bagism was ice cold, obscure, too strange, too weird. No one appeared interested in the idea. Bagism was mentioned less and less and had almost disappeared from the Bed-In discussions in spite of the hefty promotional effort John and Yoko had originally put behind it.

★ ★ ★

After a two-hour wait, the draft resisters and deserters were finally summoned to the Bed-In room by Derek. I stayed in the background as the quiet observer/producer.

At first, nobody seemed to know what to do. All the hipness evaporated from the guests. It looked like the beginnings of an elementary school dance until John Lennon focused on the baby and began to ask the others their names and where they were from. That did the trick.

Soon, everyone was crowding around the bed, getting their photos taken by John the Photographer and the kid from *Logos* magazine while the Lennons' two-man film crew filmed the session.

Grant's baby was an instant hit with John Lennon, and he was soon bottle-feeding her. He appeared very comfortable with the child.

Soon, someone asked John Lennon his general feelings about violence, and he was quick to explain he was unequivocally against all violence. When pressed for an alternative, he again invoked Gandhi as he had in other interviews.

He generously and thoughtfully told his new audience that he supported and recognized the contribution to peace and non-violence that
the draft resisters and deserters were making and admitted he would
have made the same choice, explaining, "Look, if the water is dangerous,
you should swim somewhere else."

"But what if the violence is imminent?" El asked in his strong British
accent.

I cringed.

"Then go somewhere else, anywhere else but where you are going to
provoke more violence," John said, apparently not noticing or caring that
our little group of Americans had been infiltrated by an Englishman.

Normally quiet, John the Photographer, who had been busy snapping
photos, cut in. "Can you accept the fact that there will be more violence in
the US? More bloodshed before we can be peaceful?"

Lennon seemed taken aback. He took a few moments before answering. "Yes," he said quietly, "I can accept the fact that there would be more
violence. But maybe there is still some way of avoiding it."

I heard a note of hope in his voice mixed with foreboding. I sensed a
genuine humbleness from John Lennon in our presence as if he thought
our efforts to avoid the war were not only honorable but brave. He was
talking to everyone in that room for those few moments like equals, like
fellow souls who were inhabiting the earth, as he had with me when we
had sat on the floor making posters.

Yoko chimed in almost gaily, almost like she was talking to a bunch of
kindergarteners on a class trip, repeating lines she had thrown out a hundred times already to others. "Make love to the cops and squares. Make
love to their wives."

She told my crew, "The trouble with the hippies and Yippies is that
they are snobs about peace. Peace belongs to everyone."

I saw frowns appear and brows furrow among the war resisters.

"If the squares can sell war, why can't we sell peace?" John Lennon
went on, repeating the same pitch he gave to everyone.

"And package it like soap," Yoko added, reverting back to script.

"If the establishment can package the Vietnam War and sell it, then
the best way for us to fight them is to package peace. Make it into a giant
Hollywood gimmick and sell it. We are using the media to deposit our

peace letters, we are using our records and even this Bed-In to sell peace," John said.

Yoko explained, "Look, we know that this Bed-In is nothing more than a gimmick. We are just two people who fell in love. Two freaks. John was from the pop world and I was avant-garde, and we both found something in each other by loving each other, faults and all. We'd like to share it. If everybody would just take the opportunity to find themselves, there wouldn't be any more violence. Sure, our Bed-In is a gimmick. We don't expect everyone to spend the week in bed. We just want everyone to be themselves."

"Yeah, and by being themselves, they'll probably find out they're not violent after all," Lennon concluded.

When he was asked the more delicate question, a question that had been thrust on the two of them by reporters with microphones since the Bed-In began—"What are you trying to do, John? Where do you fit in?"— he stopped, smiled. He spoke softly, intimately again. "Right now I feel like I'm running behind a big truck that's dumping a lot of shit all over the road. Most of us have accepted it and just sort of plod along through it. I guess I'm trying to catch up with the driver of that truck and tell him to stop." His sincerity came through very personal and up close.

It was also by far the best explanation of the Bed-In that I had heard.

Derek came in and told John and Yoko the time with our group was up. Derek had a TV news crew from New York in the wings.

The conference with the draft resisters and deserters ended on a positive note with a lot of "good lucks" and "hope to see you again sometime." Someone made a joke on the way out about how John and Yoko were trying so hard to get into the US when we were trying to stay out. John and Yoko laughed with us.

✫ ✫ ✫

Most of the others went home. I stayed on as did Grant, his wife, and their baby, and one or two others from my motley crew.

More people came and went, and John and Yoko were back on the phone as the TV crew from WNEW-TV in New York set up their equipment in the Bed-In room. The crew was led by producer, Ted Kavanau who told me years later that he had accompanied the younger members of his crew to the Bed-In to make sure that their coverage wasn't just a love fest but real news. [39] During the WNEW-TV interview—which turned into a documentary and aired the following week—John and Yoko were asked about how they would make peace with Fascists and people like Hitler. Yoko wisecracked that all she needed was ten days in bed with Hitler to straighten him out.

I waited until Derek had a free moment, and asked him how my meeting had gone.

"Very well. The baby was a particularly nice touch," he said, giving me a very tired smile. "John seemed quite pleased. You did a good job."

During the TV interview, I caught Derek watching a stunning young redhead. She had come into the room with the film crew. She was arguably one of the most beautiful women who had ventured into the Bed-In. Although dressed casually, her clothes were expensive. I half-expected her to ask some of the questions along with the other interviewers. Instead she remained silent, watching everyone, seemingly taking everything in.

Derek caught me watching her and smiled.

"Beautiful looking woman," I said.

"Yes, she is that."

I tried reading his expression but couldn't.

"You think you might have time for a bite to eat after this? If you want I could stay and help out."

"Tonight doesn't look good, but I promise, tomorrow we'll have a nice quiet dinner together."

I hung around for the rest of the TV interview and then did my usual rounds of the Pub, Boiler Room, and Don Juan on the way home. Ben Apfelbaum, it turned out, could not keep a secret. Every other person I ran into knew I had been at the Bed-In. People I was only casually acquainted with asked me if I could get them in.

So what was the Bed-in all about, I wondered as I finally walked home, working mentally on the article I was about to write for the *Sunday Express*.

As soon as I arrived home, I dashed off a dozen pages of notes and impressions while it was all still very fresh in my mind. I had been typing up notes since the first night, but my thoughts were still jumbled.

Where did this little moment in history fit? World peace and ending the war were competing with a lot of other pressing concerns at any given moment. Any sane person also knew we should be saving the planet from toxic pollution and environmental destruction. We should be righting the disparity between the rich and poor, and finding God, nirvana, and enlightenment. We needed to solve the racial, cultural, and social conflicts in the Middle East, Quebec, the ghettos of America, and hundreds of other hot spots around the world. We should be supporting abortion, equal rights for women, sexual freedom, throwing off the shackles of lingering seventeenth-century Puritanism, legalizing pot, and denouncing authoritarian regimes—all while earning a living, paying the rent, trying to eat healthy, exercising, finding someone to love, and worrying about the bomb, VD, unwanted pregnancy, bad trips, rip-off artists, and other evils and potential dangers and apocalypses of our times.

I wrote about the meaning of peace and violence in the context of god and no god, of sanity and insanity, and the ideals of love and the reality of pain and the pain of reality, then pushed those thoughts aside and wrote a straight journalistic piece about marketing peace like soap and about the conversations between John Lennon and the draft resisters and deserters.

John Lennon needed the war resisters to validate him. We needed him to validate us.

I felt I had the makings of a story by the time I went to bed that night.

My spirits were high.

Stupid me. It hadn't ever occurred to me that Colin Gravenor might have changed his mind about my assignment.

CHAPTER 45

"THERE'S BEEN TOO much coverage of the Bed-In already. It's not news anymore," Colin Gravenor told me when I called him early Friday morning to tell him my article was nearly complete.

"But what about the war resister angle?"

"Did you get anything new?"

I told him about the meeting and read him some quotes.

"It sounds too much like everything else the Lennons have already said. If I run anything, it'll be a photo and caption as filler. Don't worry. I'll make it up to you. There's always another story."

I hung up realizing I had just learned another lesson about publicity. You can have too much of it.

I was disappointed I had failed another assignment, but I was also re-lieved that I no longer had the deadline hanging over me.

I still had the remains of my job with Ivan. Jean-Claude said he'd likely have more work for me down the road. Guy said he was interested in reading the treatment I had given to Zeke's producer. Guy said he might even have a little money for script development once we finished the fly-ing saucer film.

I went to see Zeke at the production office on St. Lawrence Boulevard. They were on the verge of signing with Paramount. The deal was still hush-hush. Zeke kept referring to the company they were partnering with as "the guys on the mountain," referring to the Paramount logo that showed a snowcapped mountain peak.

The producer also seemed glad to see me. "I was going to call you. I finished reading *Mourning Flowers*. It's a nice, tight crime film. We should talk about turning it into a script."

He said the money to develop it would come once the Paramount deal closed.

* * *

Ivan was working away as usual when I arrived.

He ordered more coffee and asked me how my conference had gone.

I gave him the highlights. As usual, he pressed me for more details. At least someone was interested, I thought. I also told him my article had been cancelled.

"That's too bad." He sounded sympathetic. "I've had more than a few articles cancelled on me over the years. Maybe you should be thinking about creating something that would be more lasting, something that you could build a career around."

"Like what?"

"I've been thinking about that. I've seen how you work. You could do well for yourself by opening the Canadian branch of the Society for the Investigation of the Unexplained."

He may have been thinking about it, but it hit me out of the blue.

"I don't know. It sounds pretty demanding to me."

"I'd be there to guide you. Think about it," he told me. "You don't have to answer right away."

I agreed to think about it. Why not? My life was pretty rocky at that moment. I wanted to believe I could make it as a freelance writer, but I was also full of doubts about earning enough to keep going. I was ready to think about anything that might lead to paying work.

He offered to teach me how to write articles, give lectures, and become a magnet for the unexplained. "The success of the Strange, Strange World Pavilion will spawn other exhibits of the same kind around North America and eventually the world," he predicted. "The appetite for the unexplained is unlimited."

Ivan's offer sounded enticing but also too vague for me. The major incentive was that Ivan seemed to be successful, maybe even rich, and certainly secure. People were willing to hire him. He wrote books and magazine articles and appeared on TV. He knew where his next meal was coming from. That was appealing. The big drawback was that I didn't believe enough in UFOs, aliens, or land and water monsters to bet my future on them.

"Think about it," he told me again when we said our goodbyes after lunch. "I consider you a real soul mate, Joseph. We could work well together. I'll make a point of telling Jean-Claude what a great help you were."

In the four days we had been working together, we had located virtually all of the known film footage of sightings of flying saucers, the Loch Ness Monster, and the Abominable Snowman. The clips would barely make a ten-minute loop.

★ ★ ★

Upstairs at the Bed-In, it was business as usual. A steady stream of media people and fans continued to flow through the suite.

I was way too early for dinner with Derek. He expected to be tied up for a few hours. I asked if I could help out, but he said, "We now have more hands than we can use. If I think of anything, I'll let you know."

I said my hellos to John and Yoko as I usually did between audience changes. They both looked and sounded a weary.

I noticed a poster that had fallen down in one corner of the room. I got some tape and fixed it again to the wall.

All-seeing, all-knowing Derek caught my eye from across the room and nodded at me with a warm smile.

In the middle of the afternoon the stunning redhead returned. This time she brought a camera and took photos of everything and everyone. I noticed Derek discreetly watching her. She moved with such grace that it was difficult to keep my eyes off her.

Derek saw me watching him, watching her. He signaled me with his hand up, palm out to be patient.

I went back and forth between the Bed-In room and the middle room a few times and finally settled on the middle room.

Half the time, it was empty, the other half, it had one or more people hanging out or waiting on deck for an audience with John and Yoko.

As messy as the Bed-In room was, the middle room was worse. It was the *dump* room that caught the overflow and heave-ho from the main arena. By Friday, it had taken on the appearance of a toxic waste dump with plates of half-eaten meals, half-filled coffee cups with cigarette butts bobbing on the surface, half-spent candles, bunches of dead and dying flowers, and newspapers strewn around on the chairs, bed, table, and dresser tops.

Looking for something to keep me busy while I waited for Derek, I invented a new task—cleaning the middle room, which was empty of visitors at that moment.

I gathered all the plates and cups, dirty napkins, and dead and dying flowers, and piled them onto the cart by the door. I placed the candles with a little life left in them, the beads and whatever else looked like gifts or salvageable items—including sections of the local dailies— into a neat stack on top of one of the dressers. That pretty much left a half-dozen issues of a weekly underground paper delivered by one of the visitors, which had been floating around the middle room for several days. The half-dozen issues had been pawed over by multitudes of readers. Many of the pages were torn. Some had food or coffee stains on them. They were beyond salvage in my opinion. So I folded them together, pressed them down into a couple of compact piles, and stuck them under a stack of plates on the top of the food cart.

A short time later, I heard the door open between the Bed-In room and the middle room. I looked up to see John coming through the doorway, walking quickly with eyes focused ahead toward the door to the third room where Kyoko and the nanny were.

Just as he was passing the food cart, he stopped and looked at the pile of papers on top.

"What's going on? What are these doing here?" he snapped as he began pulling the copies from under the plates I had piled on them to weigh them down.

"I was just trying to clean the place," I said going to his side. Uh-oh, I thought, I've fucked up. "They're pretty grungy," I ventured, trying to find a credible excuse for messing up.

"We don't want to throw these away," he said, his face and voice softening as soon as he realized I was responsible for the near catastrophe. "We're saving them."

"Okay." I watched him carry the copies he'd salvaged from the tray to a side table and begin smoothing them out. When he was sure no more issues were lying about, he went to the closet, pulled a suitcase off the top shelf, stashed the newspapers on top of the neatly folded, clean clothes in the suitcase, and stuck the case back on the shelf in the closet.

"They can take the cart away now," he said. As he continued in the direction he had been going, he gave me a cheeky smile that told me everything was all right again.

I had to laugh when I realized how worried I was because I'd pissed off the boss.

I was still basking in good humor a half hour later when Derek showed up looking very somber.

"I need to speak with you," he said, sitting in the chair beside me, frowning, and lowering his voice even though we were the only ones in the room. I wondered if I was about to be fired.

CHAPTER 46

DEREK'S FROWN HAD nothing to do with the soiled newspapers.

"We think we know who one of the CIA infiltrators is," he told me.

"Really? Who?"

"The redhead."

"The one taking all the photos? The good looking one?" I thought he was joking.

He nodded. "John's certain she's a spy. I agree. We'd like your help."

"Me?"

"Her name's Mette Campbell. She showed up here under odd circumstances yesterday attached to the New York TV crew from WNEW. She doesn't work for them. She returned today with a camera. She's photographing everything—walls, dresser tops, floors, and everyone who comes in or out. She claims to be Norwegian-Canadian. She says she's affiliated with a Norwegian magazine that no one's ever heard of. She's been making too many jokes about pot, almost like she's hoping someone might produce a joint. I'm sure she's never worked as a journalist before."

"What do you want me to do?"

"We're keeping an eye on her. Tonight when you and I go out, we're going to take her along. She'll be your date. Talk with her. See what you think."

"I don't know, Derek."

"You'd be doing us a big favor."

A counterspy for John, Yoko, and Derek. It sounded about as nutty as everything else that had happened that week.

"Okay. What do you want me to do?"

"Just talk to her. And listen to what she says. Don't worry. I'll be there, too."

✯ ✯ ✯

Mette, the striking redhead I had noticed the previous night and that afternoon, could definitely fit the James Bond portrait of a female movie star spy.

I was quite happy to be Mette's escort since she was not only a delight to look at but warm, friendly, and easy-going, not at all my idea of a CIA operative, but then what did I know?

Or was that the point? Was her charm how she disarmed us?

Derek made reservations for us at the renowned Beaver Club, one of the best restaurants in Montreal. It also happened to be in the Queen Elizabeth Hotel. It was only an elevator ride away.

Derek's date was one of the other unsung heroes of the Bed-In, Kyoko's nanny, a quiet, dark-haired, local girl in her early twenties.

Mette seemed far more interested in talking with me about my writing, with the nanny about her studies, and with Derek about his children than John and Yoko and the Bed-In. Derek had a slew of children. Mette had a young daughter, currently at home with Mette's husband in the suburbs.

Her accent, she told us, was Norwegian. She was born in Norway and had been in Canada a few years. Her husband was Canadian. She was a model and actress.

"How did you get into the Bed-In?" I asked.

"I was in a few beer commercials for Carling," she said. Carling was a large Canadian brewery, which produced brands like Black Label and Red Cap. "The commercials aired at hockey games and baseball games for the Montreal Expos." The Montreal Expos were the newly launched National League, Eastern Division expansion team, and the first Canadian major league baseball team. The Expos had just played their inaugural game the previous month.

"I love baseball. It's the best team sport in the world," she said, eyes sparkling. Derek smiled and lifted his eyebrows in a way that made me wonder if he had ever seen a game. Mette went on to explain that she had gone to New York when the Expos played against the Mets as part of the

Carling promotional gig. "I met Ted Kavanau there. We got along famously. He's a real sweetheart. When he decided to come to Montreal to cover the Bed-In, he called me and invited me to join them."

"Have you ever worked as a photographer before?" Derek asked.

"No, but I love taking photos. And I've been in front of the camera professionally since I've been modeling and acting. I thought it would be fun to photograph the Bed-In. I'm going to offer the photos to a Norwegian magazine since they don't have anyone covering the event."

Hardly the stuff of a James Bond vixen, I thought.

Derek asked her more about the magazine and its audience, and I suspect he filed the information away in his incredible memory to check it at some future time.

I had been concentrating as much on Mette's story as I had on Derek's reaction. He took it all in, giving her a hundred percent of his attention, but I couldn't tell if he believed her or not.

I asked him what he thought when the two women went to the powder room together.

"I don't know," he said. "The one thing I am sure of is that we're being watched. The Americans would like nothing better than to come up with another excuse to keep John out of the US."

The women were gone a long time. Derek asked me again what I thought of the Bed-In. "Tell me what you really think," he insisted.

I explained not only what I heard on the street but also the kind of ambivalence I was feeling. On the one hand, John and Yoko seemed to be promoting peace, but it was difficult to separate that from their record promotions. "It seems like most of the attention is on John, the celebrity. I'm not sure the message of peace is getting anywhere except with the people who are already into it."

"What would you suggest?"

"I haven't a clue except to keep going."

John and Yoko were putting in a valiant effort. I was grateful. I wanted them to succeed, regardless of motives or potential marketing payback for their music and art. If they moved the war off the front page of some newspapers and replaced it with peace for even a day that was an achievement. "The only way to make spaceship earth work is to figure out what we can take on the spaceship and what we need to leave behind," I said, channeling Stevenson, McLuhan, Fuller, and Bob Russel. "Seems like we'll need to leave violence behind to make it work."

The evening ended soon after the women returned from the washroom. I said good night to Derek and the nanny. I walked Mette to her car. She gave me her business card, and we promised to stay in touch. As far as I knew, she drove home to her husband and young daughter in the suburbs though it was possible, I told myself, that she could have gone instead to some bunker deep in the city to hand over her film and report to the CIA on the goings on at the Bed-In.

After almost a week of chasing flying saucers, taking art lessons from John Lennon, hanging out at the Bed-In, and hunting spies, little would have surprised me. [40]

CHAPTER 47

I POPPED IN a few more times to the Bed-In but didn't stay long. The number of visitors who did stay kept increasing. John and Yoko seemed to feed off the crowd.

By the weekend, the ongoing media event had attracted a handful of celebrities— some bruised, some downright angry, and some plainly bordering on crazy. They included US comedian and civil rights activist, Dick Gregory, who had recently run unsuccessfully for Mayor of Chicago and President of the US. He wanted to enlist the Lennons in a strange scheme to end capital punishment—by broadcasting real footage of a man dying in an electric chair at Christmas time.

Singer and comedian Tommy Smothers came and stayed for several days. He was still smarting from the recent cancellation of his and his brother's groundbreaking TV show *The Smothers Brothers Comedy Hour.* It had been taken off the air because of his support for the anti-war movement and fights with his network censors. He was there to lend whatever support he could to end the war.

Timothy Leary, LSD guru, and recently declared candidate for Governor of California on a platform heavy on sex, drugs, and rock 'n' roll, was there because John Lennon had called him in New York and asked him to come. Leary had just beaten one major drug charge and was facing another.

Retired Toronto rabbi, Abraham Feinberg, a one-time opera singer and active anti-war advocate who had visited Ho Chi Minh in Hanoi, stopped by and gave John Lennon some of the ideas for a song John had been toying with throughout the Bed-In called "Give Peace a Chance."

Al Capp, a well-known virulent anti-hippie, anti-love generation American cartoonist and writer, came from the States to openly mock John and Yoko and the Bed-In and nearly ended up in a fistfight with Derek.

Allen Ginsberg continued to keep in contact by phone. Although he is listed in the lyrics of "Give Peace a Chance", he never did make it to the Bed-In. Nor did Norman Mailer, contrary to some rumors.

I was told that singer Petula Clark did make it to the Bed-In but did not make it to the recording session that produced "Give Peace a Chance." I never saw her. Nor did I see New York disc jockey and music promoter Murray the K, who called himself the fifth Beatle and befriended the Beatles early in their career. He made it to the Bed-In but not for the recording session on Saturday night. [41]

During the weekend, Timothy Leary talked with John about Leary's run for the California governorship. When John asked how he could help, Tim suggested John write a campaign song that explained his campaign slogan "Come Together, Join the Party." John loved it and immediately set about writing, "Come together, right now." He gave Leary a tape of this version of a song, which would be altered and released as a single in another version by the Beatles several months later.

I got a call from Derek on Tuesday morning. He wanted to thank me for the help I'd given him. They were leaving soon, He was wondering if I would be dropping by. I had an early meeting at Jean-Claude's studio but I said I could make a detour.

The rooms looked seedier than the last time I'd been there. Some of the bedding had been scraped off the beds. John and Yoko were on the phone or signing the remaining handmade posters that had survived the Bed-In. Many had already been given away during the past week. A couple of young women were sitting quietly in a corner just watching John and Yoko. A maid with her vacuum roaring away sucked cigarette butts out of the carpet in the adjoining room.

John wanted me to have some of the posters that we had drawn and that John and Yoko were busily signing.

I was pleased to see in the collection my own poster, *La guerre est fini* [sic], now autographed by both John and Yoko with John's trademark doodle of Yoko and John in the upper right-hand corner. I had to leave to make my appointment. I left with my own poster and a few others, telling them that I would send someone later to pick up the rest.

Le Bed-In est finie, I thought. Life after America had turned into quite a ride. What I didn't know was that John and Yoko had one last surprise for me.

CHAPTER 48

ABOUT A WEEK after the Bed-In ended, John the Photographer phoned me. He had received a verbal green light from one of the editors at *Esquire* magazine to buy some of his Bed-In photos. The catch was that *Esquire* only wanted them if he could also deliver a four-thousand-word story. "Would you be interested?"

"Of course," I said without hesitating. I was back on the street, hustling for any odd bit of writing work to keep me afloat. An *Esquire* credit would be a real score. They also paid well.

The pressure was on. I needed to write fifteen really good pages in less than forty-eight hours, and I was doing it on spec. If I didn't perform, we were dead.

With my notes and my aborted story for the *Sunday Express*, I threw myself into the task of turning a local story into an international one.

As I hastily cut, pasted, and stapled various versions together for my final draft, I made a few small errors. For the record, John and Yoko's first stop on their flight to the Bed-In was the Bahamas, not Bermuda, as I wrote. [42]

I included a short version of drawing posters with John Lennon and introducing him to the idea of *La guerre est fini [sic]*. I didn't mention the recording of "Give Peace a Chance" in my article, because I wasn't there when the song was actually recorded, and when I heard about it, I thought it was just one more gimmick in a sea of gimmicks.

I titled my article, "Seven Days in Bed with a Beatle."

It was a good first draft. I felt satisfied it was ready for editing. Just as I was getting ready to send it to *Esquire*, I got a call from John the Photographer. "*Esquire's* cancelled the article. The editor said, the Bed-In's *passé*. The world's moved on." [43]

I thought that was the end of the Bed-In for me, but John the Photographer kept calling everywhere. Within a few days, he sold the story to *Cavalier* magazine, another respectable men's magazine with nude women and top-flight articles and fiction, not quite in league with *Esquire* or *Playboy*, but with writers like Paul Krassner, Isaac Asimov, Ray Bradbury, Thomas Pynchon, and Morris Lurie. We would be paid for the photos and story in July. [44]

My article "Seven Days in Bed with a Beatle" appeared in the November issue of *Cavalier* and hit the newsstands across North America at the beginning of October. I got some satisfaction from seeing my name on the same magazine cover as Paul Krassner, but the Bed-In was already ancient news. No one cared except my mother, who bought a half-dozen copies of the racy men's magazine and showed them proudly to all the relatives who thought I was going to ruin my life by going to Canada.

Even the song, "Give Peace a Chance" had disappeared from the airwaves. It had been released on July 7 in the US and peaked at number fourteen on the US Billboard Chart over the summer in America. The first US troop withdrawals from Vietnam began on the same day.

The world had indeed moved on. Since the Bed-In, Senator Ted Kennedy, the flag bearer of the anti-war movement, had driven off an unlit bridge in Martha's Vineyard and drowned his young lady passenger under mysterious circumstances. We'd watched Neil Armstrong become the first man to walk on the moon. Woodstock, a concert and gathering in upstate New York, brought together some of the greatest bands of the decade for one last Love-In. The Zodiac killer tore through Northern California, and unknown killers—later identified as Charles Manson and his followers—butchered movie stars and rich people in Los Angeles.

***

I wanted to believe that Nixon would speed up the withdrawals and soon end the war. What I didn't know was that Nixon was reducing the troops in Vietnam to calm the public at home and at the same time, escalating the war in Southeast Asia by secretly ordering bombings and troops into Cambodia to demonstrate to the delegates at the Paris Peace Conference how tough he really was.

My mother was excited about the major televised speech President Nixon was to give on the eve of the 1969 state elections in November. She wondered whether Nixon would finally reveal the details of his "secret plan" for getting us out of Vietnam. The Nixon Doctrine, which became public on July 25, called for military and economic aid to countries fighting Communism but ground wars would be avoided, self-sufficiency of local militaries encouraged, and support would come mainly in the future from US technical aid and US air support to ensure national security of friendly nations.

Family friend Billy was wounded several more times and earned a slew of medals and promotions. I breathed a sigh of relief when I learned from my mother that his tour of duty in Vietnam had finally ended. By the time he arrived home that summer, he had won three Purple Hearts, a couple of Bronze Stars, his sergeant's stripes, and the respect of everyone who had served with him.

On September 16, two weeks after North Vietnamese President Ho Chi Minh died in office of a heart attack at age 79, Nixon ordered the withdrawal of another 35,000 soldiers from Vietnam and reduced calls for the draft. We still knew nothing about Cambodia.

Nixon's promised speech on November 3 on the eve of the state elections turned out to be nothing more than a plea for support from the part of the electorate he called for the first time "the great silent majority of my fellow Americans." His "silent majority" speech asked America to simply trust him. He claimed that was the secret to winning at the Paris Peace talks. [45]

***

The peace movement came out in full force in the middle of November for a march on Washington, DC. [46]

The November 15 march, which attracted somewhere between 200,000 and a million mainly peaceful demonstrators, was the largest single demonstration against the Vietnam War. [47]

A few days before the November 15 march, folk singer and peace activist, Pete Seeger, heard someone at a small gathering sing a catchy little ditty called "Give Peace a Chance," John Lennon's song from the Bed-In. Seeger introduced it in his set at the moratorium, saving it from oblivion, and getting everyone to sing along with him, turning it into the anti-war movement's anthem.

Just before the November 15 march, Seymour Hersh, a freelance journalist, broke one of the most powerful stories of the Vietnam War—the My Lai Massacre. The story appeared on November 13 in the *St. Louis Post-Dispatch*. The day after the march, the US Army publicly acknowledged the massacre for the first time. The atrocities had taken place a year and a half before in two villages and had left hundreds of noncombative women, children, and elderly dead and wounded. [48] [49]

When my mother asked me to step forward and come up with ideas on how to fix the world, I wrote back, "The irony of what we are caught up in can be seen in the My Lai massacres. Each one of us is taking the chance of being a war criminal."

I hated the idea that I could get caught up in a machine that could make me do whatever it pleased, even commit war crimes. I also felt a kinship with the soldier, the sick soldier, the deranged soldier, the soldier under orders who simply could get caught up in something as horrible as My Lai. The military was about following orders. It was about having your individual will, your individual ability to reason beaten out of you so that you act as a killing machine in battle. I continued to feel helpless in the wake of the war and the ongoing violence in the US and Canada. [50] [51]

Alice returned briefly. She still had a key to my place. She returned every night for about a week, coming and going as she pleased, and then disappeared again. Later, I heard she'd become engaged to some older man who owned a clothing factory. Sarah found steady work with a traveling light show for rock concerts. Bar owner Johnny Vago introduced me to a wonderful and wonderfully messed up heiress with a young child who was in the midst of a messy divorce. We lived together for a few months in a beautiful cottage along the Ottawa River, an hour out of town by train. The relationship was doomed from the start. She was determined to distance herself from her wild-child past and move to the States where I was still wanted by the FBI.

Zeke's film and his marriage fell apart at the same time. He was devastated. I spent a lot of time consoling him, trying to lift his spirits. He talked a lot about moving to Toronto where he was originally from. He wanted me to go, too. I told him I wasn't ready yet.

I finally got a paid assignment from Colin Gravenor for the *Sunday Express*—a feature story about hunger and poverty in Montreal. I filled it with statistics and interviewed the heads of several social agencies. Colin gave me a full-page on page five on June 29, 1969 under my by-line with three photos I had taken with a borrowed camera. It ran with the headline: "Hunger fact of life for thousands."

Guy started shopping my film treatment around to small local film companies.

I rented half my place to Jerry, a young photo lab guy, to cut the rent in half. Jerry and his friends were experimenting with magic and wizardry on the side. They soon turned my apartment into a happy-go-lucky den for young, crazy, stoned, wannabe magicians, who were more amusing than dangerous or sinister.

✳ ✳ ✳

The first lottery for conscription for the Vietnam War was held on December 1, 1969. It was the first draft lottery since World War II. My number was 179, probably high enough to get me exempted if I hadn't already been drafted and indicted. The lottery did nothing to dampen the anti-draft sentiments inside the States. More Americans left for Canada.

✳ ✳ ✳

A couple of weeks later, on a cold, damp day in the middle of December, while walking along St. Catherine Street, contemplating the start of my third winter in Montreal, I happened to look up and notice a billboard on the top of a building hovering over the downtown. It said simply:

"WAR IS OVER!

"IF YOU WANT IT

"Happy Christmas from John & Yoko"

La guerre est finie.

I was stunned in a good way. John and Yoko had taken an idea that I had borrowed from a movie house marquee and had added their own spin—"*If you want it.*" They put it on a billboard in Montreal only a few blocks from where I had drawn posters with John Lennon. Billboards with the same message had gone up in cities around the world. [52 53]

Far out. Fucking far out, I thought as I laughed out loud.

I felt a weird sense of redemption and validation.

I wondered if John or Yoko remembered me. They had met so many people. Maybe John did.

It didn't matter. The message was the point. Stop the war. Stop all war.

I was the accidental messenger. I had passed the words onto someone who could do something with them.

Life after America, war is over, peace, love, and hope, all wrapped together. The choice was simple. The bomb or spaceship earth. Armageddon or world peace. I'd made my choice. I was satisfied I'd done the right thing. [54]

An enhanced image (with spelling errors) of the original drawing of *La guerre est fini* [sic]—*War Is Over*—drawn by Joseph Mark Glazner while working alongside John Lennon on the first day of the weeklong Montreal Bed-In for Peace, May 27, 1969. The poster can be seen in many photos and films of the Bed-In. "War Is Over...if you want it" became a central theme of the Lennons' peace initiative at the end of 1969. ©Joseph Mark Glazner.

Acknowledgments

I would like to acknowledge and thank the following people who spoke or corresponded with me, encouraged me, read early versions of *Life After America*, offered suggestions, or helped in other ways as I researched, wrote, and edited this memoir over the past decade:

Al Abramson, Salem Alaton, Louise Aronoff, Leslie Asplund, Rosemary Aubert, Rupert Auchterlonie, Paul Azzaria, Jeffery Beach, John Beck, David Beckett, Bruce Beery, Karen Beery, Shulamit Beigel, Susan Belany, Guy Bergeron, Stephen Borsuk, Michel Brault, Nathan Bress, Charles Brown, Sam Brody, Richard Brownell, Lynda Butler, Mette Campbell, Daniel Couvreur, Larissa Covato, Brian Cullman, Nancy Daubney, Barbara Dinger, Barbara Dodge, Jacky Donovan, James Dubro, Alex Dukay, Larry Duprey, Jock Ferguson, Michel Fortier, Rudy Franchi, Raymond Fraser, Richard Glanville-Brown, Alan Glazner, Linda Glazner, Raymond Glazner, Robert Glazner, Kristian Gravenor, Richard Grigonis, Helaine Golan, Terry Guerin, Terry Haig, Madeleine Harris-Callway, Uno Hoffmann, Charles Hollander, Barbara Holzmark, Mark Howell, Fred Jordan, Shane Joseph, Susan Joyce, Ted Kavanau, Roy Kerwood, Dan Kramon, Kay Kramon, Paul Krassner, Bill Kurchak, Max Layton, Julian Lebensold, Peter Lebensold, Lucien LeComte, Iris Leigh, Miriam Leigh, Nathan Leigh, William Leigh, Larry Lusko, Chip Madinger, D.J. McIntosh, Earl Manners, Paul D. Marks, Clare Mian, Cindy Mills, Georges Monette, Christopher G. Moore, John Morthland, Stephen Overbury, Trixi Rittenhouse, Carol Rusoff, Garry Rusoff, Robert Russel, Randy Saharuni, Baiba St. John, Richard St. John, Joann Sason, Alicia Scarth, Debbie Sharp, Joanie Shirriff, Ross Skoggard, Eric Slone, John Sullivan, Betty Ann Tutching, John Vader, Elizabeth Vihnanek, Michael Vosse, Alfie Wade, Jr., Diane Wanat, June Weber, Cindy Weiss, Jeff Weiss, Jon Wolfe, and others who I unintentionally may have missed.

Special thanks to Erin Linn McMullan (editor).

Notes

CHAPTER 2

[1] Paul Krassner's satire in *The Realist* (reprinted several months later by the *McGill Daily*) contained several pages allegedly left out of William Manchester's biography of President Kennedy, *The Death of a President*. Some pages of the bestseller had been left out after Jacqueline Kennedy sued Manchester's publisher, resulting in a settlement to remove certain parts of the book. Writing in a style that mimicked Manchester, Krassner wrote his controversial piece of twenty fake paragraphs under the headline, "The Parts That Were Left Out of the Kennedy Book." The content was vile, aimed at demonizing President Johnson, showing him having sex with JFK's corpse on the plane back from Dallas after JFK's assassination. When asked about the satire, Krassner defended it by comparing it to Johnathan Swift's shocking satire on ways to cook and eat Irish children as a means to combat poverty.

[2] I met Paul Krassner over the summer of 1967 while he was still embroiled in the controversy following his crude attack on President Johnson in the May issue of *The Realist*. Krassner was a true anti-war hero and among the first to expose the US's deep involvement in the Vietnam War. *The Realist's* hard-hitting, groundbreaking articles on Vietnam forced the mainstream media to take a close and critical look at the war for the first time. *The Realist* had also been the first newspaper to publish a detailed article on the US internment camps and the laws on the books that made it possible for the US government to round up and incarcerate dissidents in time of war. This government list was supposed to have my name on it—most likely because nearly a dozen of my friends in four different incidents between 1966-67 had been busted for drugs, including some at the center of the music industry, which was increasingly being viewed by the establishment as a political and subversive force in America.

CHAPTER 6

[3] The term "separatist" is widely used inside and outside Quebec by those who are opposed to Quebec leaving Canada and forming a separate country. Those who are in favor of Quebec leaving Canada refer to themselves as sovereignists or nationalists.

CHAPTER 8

[4] After the Viet Minh and its Vietnamese allies pushed the French Colonials out of their country, the new united country was supposed to hold a referendum in two years to determine who would govern. US President Eisenhower, backed by other democracies and Eisenhower's advisers from the military-industrial complex inside the

US, feared the Communists would win a fair election. They instead opted to partition the country and helped install a minority Catholic president in a majority Buddhist (and Communist) country to head South Vietnam, denying a nationwide election. I believe Eisenhower's farewell address as President in 1961, where he warned America of the military-industrial complex, in part, reflects his disillusionment over the advice he had been given on Vietnam.

CHAPTER 9

[5] Gilles Carle, Claude Jutra, Michel Brault, and a handful of others were the vanguard of a new wave of young Québécois filmmakers, most of whom passed through the French section of the National Film Board in the 1950s and early 1960s, and were inventing Quebec cinema in the late 1960s. This small group of men were schooled in all aspects of filmmaking, and in some cases, used the pretense of making documentaries to shoot rogue low-budget feature films while at the NFB.

[6] Both Claude Jutra and Michel Brault had a major influence on international filmmaking at the time. Each had gone to Paris and worked with some of the rising stars there. Jutra worked with Francois Truffaut on *Anna la bonne*. Brault shot some of the scenes for Jean Rouch's *Chronicles of a Summer (Chronique d'un été)* where Brault introduced the French director to a style of cinematography that he and Jutra, and others, had been playing with. The new style, called *Cinéma Direct* (Direct Cinema), relied heavily on the Arriflex camera and the Nagra recorder, which could be synchronized. The new portable equipment could be operated by one person and allowed filmmakers to more accurately capture the reality of a scene. Direct Cinema became synonymous with *cinéma vérité*, or truthful cinema. While Jean Rouch, the French director most closely associated with *cinéma vérité*, gave Brault and the NFB credit for pioneering it, Brault and most of his Québécois colleagues continued to call their work *Cinéma Direct*.

[7] During the years of our friendship, some of the artists Suzelle gave a start, or an early boost, to their careers and who become internationally acclaimed, included Italian-born Vittorio Fiorucci; the one-armed, Catalan-born painter, ceramist, and sculptor, Jordi Bonet; the Romanian-born, Jewish sculptor and painter, Sorel Etrog; Quebec sculptor Armand Vaillancourt, husband of Suzanne Verdal, *the Suzanne* in Leonard Cohen's song "Suzanne," Montreal artist and printmaker, Michel Fortier, and his wife, artist Trixi Rittenhouse.

CHAPTER 11

[8] *Take One* was published sporadically with no dates on the cover so the magazines could be sold on newsstands forever, like a book. The articles came from filmmakers,

critics, and global thinkers from the US, Canada, and Europe. The publishing and editorial office was a small space on the lower floor of the building owned by Peter's father, Fred Lebensold, beside Suzelle Carle's Boutique Soleil in Vieux Montreal.

[9] "A Thousand Spring Soldiers" by Joseph Mark Glazner, Montreal, copyright 1968-2017

> A thousand spring soldiers in green,
> camouflaged to avoid being seen.
> From winter to fall they march and sing,
> killing each other for their own shade of green.
>
> Chorus:
> But green is better on leaves,
> And leaves are better on trees.
>
> They trample the earth, spilling their blood,
> turning lush meadows to sores of brown mud,
> The last leaves laugh dryly a warning to men
> though their voices are weak in the breeze:
>
> Go home, go home, foolish men—
> Iron shall rust and soldiers shall freeze.
> No battle against time can be won,
> Not even by men dressed as trees.
>
> Look to the sun, it sets in the west;
> Winter is long, all shall be lost,
> But no one heeded the whispering leaves,
> So the frost turned fall soldiers to dust.

CHAPTER 12

[10] Robert Stanfield's family had made a fortune in textiles and was best known for its brand of men's underwear sold under the Stanfield's label, a company that had developed unshrinkable underwear in 1898 and owned a 1915 patent for two-piece adjustable Long Johns.

CHAPTER 13

[11] Directed by Alain Resnais and released in 1966, *La guerre est finie* was already a couple of years old in 1968-69 when I first ran into the title.

CHAPTER 14

[12] Although a Torontonian and raised in English Canada, Russel had lived for a number of years in Paris and Montreal and had been the theater critic for the CBC, focusing on the French Theater scene in Montreal, before and after becoming a filmmaker. He had an unaccredited voice-over part in Claude Jutra's *À tout prendre* and had made two of his own films with Jutra and Michel Brault, and one with Robert Hershorne (also spelled Hirschhorn and Hershorn), Leonard Cohen's close friend. Hershorne had turned Russel onto pot, and Cohen onto pot and even harder drugs. Hershorne died under mysterious circumstances in Hong Kong in the early 1970s—some said from an overdose of heroin while others said he was a murder victim whose dismembered body was found in a suitcase, the victim of a drug deal gone wrong.

[13] Robert Russel had already launched the first version of his information service and had been shut down by *The New York Times* over copyright issues before I arrived. The new service he was trying to launch was an attempt to commercially resurrect his concept in a new form that skirted the copyright laws.

CHAPTER 16

[14] Matthias Kunheim, sometimes spelled Kuenheim, was the third of four children and the second son of Dr. Hugo and Brigitte von Kunheim. Hugo was a wealthy German industrialist with Jewish roots. Matt's mother, Brigitte Helm, (born Brigitte Eva Gisela Schittenhelm) played the dual role of Maria and the machine-human character in Fritz Lang's 1927 silent film classic, *Metropolis*. Brigitte and Hugo left Germany around 1935 in protest over Hitler's policies and became residents of Switzerland where Matt was born in 1938.

CHAPTER 17

[15] In 1965, when Russel was about to incorporate his first company, he turned to Marshall McLuhan—who, by then, Russel referred to as Uncle Marshall—and asked him what he should call his company. In a playful mood, McLuhan, a devoted Roman Catholic, told him with a wave his hands as if giving a Papal blessing, "You be in Orbis," a takeoff on "Urbis et Orbis," meaning "to the city of Rome and the World," the standard opening for speeches during the Roman Empire and later used to indicate Papal addresses and Apostolic Blessings.

CHAPTER 19

[16] The Yippies—for Youth International Party—was founded during a New Year's gathering (December 31, 1967) at the New York apartment of Abbie and Anita Hoffman by both Hoffmans, Jerry Rubin, and his long-time girlfriend, Nancy Kurshan, and Paul Krassner. Krassner claimed to have coined the term Yippie, a takeoff on hippie, and then created the full name for the movement—the Youth International Party— to match the first three letters of Yippee. The Yippies were supposed to symbolize a growing radicalization between the peace-love-dope hippie-freaks and the more politically conscious, anti-war and increasingly radicalized youth. The Yippie flag was a black background with a marijuana leaf over a red, five-pointed star in the center.

The Yippie movement promoted a "New Nation" concept, supported by free health clinics, urban and rural communes, underground publications, food co-operatives, legal aid, and general support for the alternate youth culture.

Part of the idea behind the Yippies as a political movement was to use humor to try to point out the absurdity of American life, formal institutions, industrialization, war, and racism. Hoffman and several others had already participated in a number of public pranks prior to the founding of the Yippies.

CHAPTER 20

[17] Along with Mount Royal in the center of Montreal and several other peaks, they made up a small chain of mountains formed by volcanic action about 125 million years ago in the St. Lawrence River Valley between the Appalachian Mountains to the south and the Laurentian Mountains to the north.

CHAPTER 24

[18] "Rifleman Is Arrested Near Nixon Apartment," *The New York Times*, November 6, 1968, p. 20. The story was circulated widely by AP.

[19] The Namers were acquitted of all conspiracy charges the following summer.

CHAPTER 25

[20] The album cover of *Unfinished Music No. 1: Two Virgins* featured John and Yoko on the cover in full frontal nudity. Because of the full frontal nudity on the cover, several places in the US pronounced the album obscene and seized copies in their jurisdiction, including New Jersey, which confiscated some 30,000 albums in January 1969.

CHAPTER 26

[21] *Midnight* and the other tabloids of the Globe had an edgy legitimacy among English writers in Montreal during the 1960s and early 1970s. The alumni included writer, TV personality, and later, city politician Nick Auf der Maur and other well-known writers, editors, and publishers for the dailies and in the book-publishing world.

CHAPTER 30

[22] Sir George Williams University became part of Concordia University in 1974.

CHAPTER 33

[23] The number of US troops in Vietnam peaked at the end of April 1969 at 543,400. By then, American fatalities in Vietnam were close to 40,000, several thousand more than American fatalities in the Korean War.

CHAPTER 36

[24] By the time I sold out, the stock dropped another ten percent. I was one of the lucky ones, recovering about half my money. IOS went to nearly zero, then zero a few years later, landing its founder, Bernie Cornfeld, in a Swiss jail on fraud charges for nearly a year. Though Cornfeld was eventually cleared, IOS was branded the great Ponzi scheme of the 1960s. I took solace in the fact that my mother hadn't listened to me and hadn't bought the fund when I had so glibly advised her to.

CHAPTER 37

[25] The Battle of Hamburger Hill, or Ap Bia Mountain, and also known as Hill 937, took place May 10-20, 1969, and resulted in the deaths of 46 US soldiers, with 400 wounded and the deaths of 633 North Vietnamese Army (NVA) combatants. It was a senseless battle, in which the Americans finally took a muddy hill against entrenched NVA soldiers, only to abandon the hill in the end. The story contributed to a growing sense the war was indeed senseless and unwinnable.

[26] In the song, John Lennon talked about being crucified and how difficult life could be. The use of the word "Christ" and his suggestion that he might be crucified got John in trouble again with some religious zealots. But that would all come days and weeks later.

CHAPTER 38

[27] Nick Knowland had filmed and narrated the voice of the rapist in 1968 for John and Yoko's 77-minute 16 mm movie *Rape*, shot at the end of 1968 and released on TV in 1969. The movie was co-produced, co-written, co-directed, and co-edited by John and Yoko. It was a Warhol-type film that showed not much more than a camera following a scared young woman around London, culminating in her rape. Mike Lax did the sound on many of John and Yoko's other productions alongside Nick Knowland.

[28] Yoko was battling her ex-husband, director Tony Cox, the father of Kyoko, over custody issues regarding their daughter.

[29] Some of the film footage, showing Yoko Ono and me working together hanging posters on the wall before the press arrived, can be seen around the five-minute mark in the John and Yoko directed and produced feature-length documentary *john & yoko, the bed-in*, also titled, *Bed Peace*. I also appear briefly in the film in the background during the session with the draft resisters and deserters at around the twenty-five-minute mark. I am wearing a yellow sport jacket and green neckerchief and sitting beside my drawing of *La guerre est fini* [sic]. Note: Many of the Bed-In events in the film are shown out of chronological order.

CHAPTER 39

[30] Ivan T. Sanderson's work in the 1930s provided much of what was known in the field at the time about the animal behavior of a number of exotic species, previously only studied in death or in captivity.

[31] The term cryptologist was later popularized by another cryptologist, Dr. Bernard Heuvelmans, a Belgian scientist who worked with Ivan and credited him with coining the term.

[32] The publication of *The Abominable Snowman* was also the point at which the mainstream scientific community began to turn its back on Ivan. Fully committed to answering whether these strange phenomena were real or not, he created The Ivan T. Sanderson Foundation at his rural pre-Revolutionary War-era colonial farmhouse on the New Jersey side of the Delaware Valley in 1965. Two years later, he turned it into the non-profit Society for the Investigation of the Unexplained.

CHAPTER 41

[33] No one will ever know how many genuine draft resisters and deserters came to Canada, stayed in Canada, left for some other country, or returned to the US during the

Vietnam War. All numbers are guesses. Bona fide draft resisters and deserters, who took up residence in Canada during the Vietnam War, probably numbered less than 25,000 spread across the entire country. I have found no credible statistics to support the higher numbers of 50,000-100,000, which came repeatedly from unsubstantiated estimates and rumors in the underground and mainstream press. The media repeated these unverified estimates so many times they became urban legends. During the Vietnam War, most military deserters most likely simply went underground in the US. Only a small portion ever left the US for a foreign country. The vast majority—possibly as high as 90 percent of draft resisters—also never left the US.

[34] Ben's father was a professor at New York University. Ben studied anthropology and worked under Margaret Mead at the Museum of Natural History for four years before coming to Montreal to avoid the draft. Ben Apfelbaum's older sister, Faith Apfelbaum Sale, was a well-regarded editor in the New York publishing world. Ben's brother-in-law, J. Kirkpatrick Sale, was a well-known writer and friend of Thomas Pynchon and Richard Farina. Farina was Sale's Cornell roommate, co-leader, and fellow arrestee in a famous student rebellion at the university in 1958.

[35] John Vago was trying to pump new life into the Don Juan, which was a dance place, rather than just a drinking hole like his other two clubs. Ben and new junior partners of Vago's, actor Peter Cullen and Peter's wife, Carol, were the new front people at the Don Juan. Peter Cullen had a large circle of friends from Westmount and his TV work. Cullen had been the announcer on *The Smothers Brothers Comedy Hour* before the network cancelled the show.

CHAPTER 42

[36] Unbeknownst to me at the time, Ivan had been at the center of a sensational story of his own for the past year. The controversy centered on the dead body of the so-called Minnesota Iceman. The Iceman was a strange creature, shot in the head, preserved in a block of ice, and reputed to be the recently deceased remains of a Neanderthal that had been living in our times.

The carcass had been displayed in a carnival-like exhibit touring Wisconsin, Illinois, and Minnesota. A zoology student contacted Ivan, and Ivan and his friend cryptologist, Dr. Bernard Heuvelmans, drove to a farm in Minnesota to view the corpse. Both scientists were convinced the dead man was the real thing—an authentic Big Foot. Both began writing scientific and popular articles on the creature. Ivan mentioned the Ice Man on the Johnny Carson show in late 1968, several months before the Bed-In.

A friend of Ivan's, a top scientist at the Smithsonian, became interested, but Heuvelmans apparently spooked the exhibitor, threatening to call the FBI, police, or other authorities if the exhibitor didn't permit him access to the body. Soon afterward the exhibitor stopped exhibiting the original creature, perhaps even burying it, and showing instead a wax model that differed considerably from measurements that Ivan originally made.

Ivan continued to claim that on his initial visit he had seen a real creature and smelled and seen other evidence of decay of what he believed were human remains. Heuvelmans later wrote a book claiming the original cadaver was a genuine, modern-day Neanderthal. He also theorized it had been killed in the jungles of Vietnam where hairy, wild, half-ape, half-human reclusive creatures were supposed to live. He believed it was smuggled stateside in a military coffin in a similar fashion as heroin was smuggled into the US during the Vietnam War.

[37] At the time we were working together, he was writing the "Invisible Residents," about underwater UFOs with mentions of the Bermuda Triangle, and "This 'Airplane' Is More Than A 1000 Years Old." These stories were scheduled for the November *Argosy* issue. The latter was breaking new ground. He was theorizing that some small gold objects found in Mayan tombs could possibly be models of ancient airplanes.

CHAPTER 43

[38] John and Yoko would later call the people who hung around the Bed-In, The Plastic Ono Band.

CHAPTER 44

[39] Ted Kavanau would later become founding producer of CNN headline news, head of CNN's first investigative reporting unit, and the winner of a number of Emmys. He also lost all his money in the stock market and would eventually co-author a book about how to get fit and find peace of mind while lying in bed.

CHAPTER 46

[40] Ivan's friend and biographer, Richard "Zippy" Grigonas has been able to establish that Sanderson was a high-ranking spook, rising to the rank of Commander for British Naval Intelligence during World War II, in charge of British naval intelligence for the Caribbean during the war, and at times, using his work as a collector of animal species as a cover. Stationed in New York City as part of the British propaganda machine during part of the war, he also operated as a liaison with intelligence officers of the Office of Strategic Services, the precursor to the CIA. Grigonas could find no evidence that Ivan still maintained ties to British or US intelligence communities during the Bed-In.

CHAPTER 47

[41] Sometime on Saturday, John decided to record his new song "Give Peace a Chance." He asked Derek to arrange for the proper sound equipment. Derek asked Richard Glanville-Brown to handle it. Richard contacted André Perry, owner of an independent studio. Perry arrived Saturday night with some rented recording equipment, capturing the first takes of "Give Peace a Chance."

CHAPTER 48

[42] Many errors have occurred in reporting on the Bed-In over the years. One persistent myth is that the Bed-In began on May 26, when in fact it began on May 27, as I describe. The Lennons were in Toronto on May 26 and didn't arrive in Montreal until around midnight.

[43] *Esquire* wasn't the only one to cancel stories on the Bed-In. *Life* magazine commissioned and paid for a series of photos by Gerry Dieter but never published them. My drawing, *La guerre est fini* [sic], appeared in a number of these photos, which were subsequently exhibited and published decades later by Dieter's estate.

[44] "Seven Days in Bed with a Beatle," by Joseph Mark Glazner, was the lead story in *Cavalier* magazine (Fawcett Publications), November 1969, pp. 28-29, 83, 88, 93-94.

[45] The November state elections were a victory for many mainly moderate Republicans, including the governor of Virginia, the first Republican to occupy that office in 84 years, and the mayor of New York City, where Republican incumbent mayor John Lindsay was forced to run and won as an independent after his own party had rejected him for being too liberal. Democrat Carl Stokes became the first African-American to win the mayoralty of a major US city when he won in Cleveland. Moderate Republican William Cahill, whom Nixon had personally campaigned for, as he had for the moderate Virginia governor, won the New Jersey governor's race, bringing the total of Republican governors to thirty-two out of fifty, a number not seen since the Eisenhower years.

[46] The official title of the November 15 march was the "November 15 National Mobilization Committee to End the War in Vietnam Moratorium." The November 15 march was a follow-up to demonstrations held on October 15. The October 15 demonstrations were called the Moratorium to End the War in Vietnam and rallies were held in cities across the world with huge crowds turning out at city centers and college and university campuses.

[47] Not on the news that night, but noteworthy was the attendance of Timothy Leary. It was the very first peace rally he had attended. He was awaiting the outcome of several different drug-related court cases against him in several jurisdictions. He went on stage with Peter, Paul, and Mary and sang "Blowin' in the Wind."

Dr. Benjamin Spock, baby doctor, author, and anti-war activist, was one of the featured speakers. He had a two-year prison sentence hanging over him for conviction on charges of blocking a Manhattan Army induction center.

[48] The My Lai story broke like a dispatch from Hell. On March 16, 1968, US troops entered My Lai and My Khe, two hamlets of the village of Son My, two months after the Tet Offensive. The US soldiers were looking for suspected Viet Cong, who they believed had retreated to Son My. Orders were to clean out the villages. The attack on the villages left between 347 and 504 dead and an unknown number injured. The casualty figures varied because no official body count was made. Many of the dead were tortured and raped, and all were unarmed civilians, including babies, children, women, and elderly.

[49] Following the revelation of My Lai and My Khe massacres, John Lennon returned his Order of the British Empire medal (MBE) to the Queen, stating he was doing so because of the British government's support of the "Nigeria-Biafra thing," the Vietnam War, and the fact that "Cold Turkey," Lennon's second solo release, was "slipping down in the charts."

[50] The violence inside the US against the war and the government continued unabated. Between January 1969 and April 1970, 3,355 incendiary and 975 explosive bombs were set off by American dissidents in the US resulting in 43 deaths, many more injuries, and an estimated $21.8 million in property damage.

[51] Violence continued to haunt Montreal, too. In June, less than two weeks after the Lennons left town, an FLQ bomb went off at the Sherbrooke Street office of the Saint-Jean-Baptiste Society, founded in 1834 and responsible for instituting the French-Canadian holiday of Saint-Jean-Baptiste as a Quebec national holiday in 1922. The organization had made the mistake of inviting Prime Minister Pierre Trudeau, a federalist and enemy of the Quebec separatists, to preside over their annual parade. It was the same parade at which the previous year Trudeau had dodged rocks and bottles. The Society's office was only two blocks from me. The explosion rattled my windows and every bone and fiber in my body.

Wow, was all I could say, when I went out on the street soon afterward. The windows at the front of the Society's building were gone. The sidewalk in front of the old Victorian stone building where the Society was headquartered was covered with glass.

The Society withdrew its invitation. Trudeau was angry. More bombs followed during the summer and fall, including one on September 29 that destroyed the home of Montreal Mayor Jean Drapeau.

[52] I knew nothing about the long and secret planning that went into John and Yoko's development of their War Is Over campaign, sprung on the world on December 15. The campaign would be called by some their second-most important collaboration after "Give Peace a Chance." Both had sprung from the Bed-In.

The War Is Over campaign was the first multi-media campaign for peace, launched with billboards in ten cities—London, Amsterdam, Montreal, Toronto, New York, Los Angeles, Paris, Rome, West Berlin, and Athens. (Tokyo was mentioned in the first press release but apparently the Tokyo billboard never went up.) The launch was simultaneously accompanied by distribution of thousands of posters and postcards in those cities, this time including Tokyo, as well as newspaper ads and radio and TV promotion.

In addition to the December 15 press release, the official launch of the campaign came later in the evening at the Peace for Christmas charity concert for UNICEF at the Lyceum Ballroom. The concert featured John and Yoko and The Plastic Ono Band—made up that evening of Eric Clapton, Klaus Voormann, and Alan White—and a stellar cast of additional performers including George Harrison, Billy Preston, Keith Moon, Bobby Keys, Jim Gordon, Delaney and Bonnie Bramlett.

[53] "Happy Xmas (War Is Over)" a song by John Lennon and Yoko Ono furthering the theme of the War Is Over campaign, was released in the US in 1971 and in the UK the following year.

[54] By the end of 1969, nearly forty-nine thousand Americans and many hundreds of thousands of Vietnamese had perished in the Vietnam War. More than nine thousand additional US soldiers would die and many thousands more would be wounded and scarred before America withdrew the last of its ground troops three years later in 1973. More than a million Vietnamese soldiers and civilians lost their lives in their civil war.

About Joseph Mark Glazner

Joseph Mark Glazner is an internationally acclaimed American-Canadian author of seven crime novels, written under his own name and his pen name, Joseph Louis, including the Shamus and Arthur Ellis nominated novel, *Madelaine*.

Glazner's first memoir, *Life After America*, is about his adventures as a young American war resister, who left the US for Canada during the wild and crazy 1960s, reinvented himself as a pulp writer, and found a small place in history helping John Lennon kick-start his "War Is Over" campaign at the iconic Montreal Bed-In for Peace in 1969.

Glazner recounts with dark humor and the eye of a thriller writer his nearly bungled escape from the US, the pitfalls of love in an era of sexual revolution, fly-by-night jobs as a new immigrant, and a stint writing tabloid stories about UFOs that killed people and sheep.

Glazner was raised in rural Warrenville, New Jersey. He earned a bachelor's degree in psychology (*magna cum laude*) from the University of Southern California and was elected to the Phi Beta Kappa Society in 1967. In addition to writing crime novels and memoirs, he has worked as a journalist, screenwriter, futurist in a think tank, and communications adviser to corporations and governments in Canada. the US, and the Bahamas.

He lives in Toronto, Canada.

Printed in Great Britain
by Amazon